CASEY WATSON

SUNDAY TIMES BESTSELLING AUTHOR

A Dark Secret

Abuse and heartache are

all Sam has ever known

HARPER
element

This book ...ences.
In ord... cs,
dial...

HarperElement
An imprint of HarperCollins*Publishers*
1 London Bridge Street
London SE1 9GF

www.harpercollins.co.uk

First published by HarperElement 2019

1 3 5 7 9 10 8 6 4 2

A catalogue record of this book is
available from the British Library

PB ISBN 978-0-00-829861-6
EB ISBN 978-0-00-829865-4

Printed and bound in Great Britain by
CPI Group (UK) Ltd, Croydon, CR0 4YY

MIX
Paper from
responsible sources
FSC™ C007454

This book is produced from independently certified FSC™ paper
to ensure responsible forest management.

For more information visit: www.harpercollins.co.uk/green

This book is dedicated to the army of passionate foster carers out there, each doing their bit to ensure that our children are kept as safe as possible in such a changing and often scary world. As technology is reinvented and becomes ever more complicated for those of us who were not brought up amid such advances, we can only try to keep up, in the hope that we continue to learn alongside our young people.

Acknowledgements

I remain endlessly grateful to my team at HarperCollins for their continuing support, and I'm especially excited to see the return of my editor, the very lovely Vicky Eribo, and look forward to sharing my new stories with her. As always, nothing would be possible without my wonderful agent, Andrew Lownie, the very best agent in the world in my opinion, and my grateful thanks also to the lovely Lynne, my friend and mentor forever.

Chapter 1

Aqua aerobics in February. In February. Had I completely lost my marbles? I couldn't remember which of my so-called friends had suggested it, but by now I was sorely regretting having agreed to it. Not only was it absolutely Baltic outside, but I had just suffered the most embarrassing incident ever, and as we huddled in our respective changing cubicles in the leisure centre (which were only marginally less Baltic) the same so-called friends – not to mention my sister Donna – were still teasing me about it relentlessly.

'Oh, Casey,' Donna said, laughing, 'such a priceless Barbara Windsor moment!'

'I must, I must, improve my bust!' my friend Kate added, gleefully.

And all I could do was take the teasing, and grin and bear it. Or should that have been 'bare' it? Definitely. It was such a basic error, after all.

Having not gone swimming in any form for a good couple of years now, I no longer had a suitable swimsuit, and given that this wasn't the time of year for 'summer holiday essentials', the stores didn't have a great deal of choice. Luckily I had spotted a sale rail and found a front-fastening, gold (of all colours) bikini. And were that not enough to mark me out as a rookie, during a rather robust arms-out-to-the side-and-do-a-windmill thrust, my all-singing, all-dancing, shimmering gold bikini had unclasped with a ping, giving me no choice but to do a duck dive, and leaving me scrabbling around under the water, trying to regain both the shreds of my bikini top and my dignity. But not before the whole class, including the instructor, had witnessed it. I was going to have to seriously rethink how I approached this whole 'me time' malarkey.

'Okay, okay,' I called out from my own changing booth. 'I'm so happy I've brightened up your morning. And I'm *so* happy that mobile phones aren't allowed in the frigging pool, either, because I can only imagine the pleasure you'd have all taken in capturing it for all time.'

Amid the ensuing laughter, as if I'd summoned it, my own phone started to ring. Delving into my changing bag – one that would put Mary Poppins to shame, obviously – I found it and saw it was a call from Christine Bolton, my still relatively new fostering link worker.

Had she called to tease me too? If so, news travelled fast. Quickly drying one side of my face, I put the phone to my ear, first explaining where I was, so she'd understand all the cackles, bumps and bangs.

'I'm surprised to hear from you again so quickly,' I added, as I parked my damp bottom on a towel slung on the wooden-slatted bench. I'd only spoken to her the day before and I knew there was nothing on the horizon. Though there had been – up until a few days ago, we'd been earmarked for a particularly difficult teenager badly in need of a calm, stable home. But as often happens in fostering, there was a game-changer. Just a day before all concerned were due in court, a grandparent had kindly stepped forward to offer to take the child in and so the case had been dropped. And to the great relief of all concerned. So we were expecting a lull now – hence all the 'me-time'. Till another long-term placement came up we were only really doing respite, and that mostly for our most recent child, Miller, who was now in a residential school and with a new primary carer, Mavis.

'I know,' Christine replied, 'and I'm so sorry to bother you in the middle of your swimming, but that mini-break you said you and Mike were hoping to jet off on – have you booked anything yet?'

I immediately wished we had, because I had a hunch I knew what was coming. A lull in the world of fostering was never guaranteed to be anything more than twenty-four hours, and more often than not it wasn't. I suspected this was the situation here – that an urgent case had presented itself. I wasn't wrong.

'No, not as yet,' I said. 'Shouldn't I?'

'Possibly not. At least, if you're up for taking a child on. D'you know Kelly and Steve Blackwell? Live out in the sticks and have two small children?'

'Indeed I do,' I said. 'And pretty well. I was Kelly's mentor for a year.'

Mentoring had always been the unofficial practice in fostering, but over the last couple of years it had become an even more important part of the process. One in which longer-term, more experienced carers were expected to take on the role of mentor to new carers just coming into the field. In my case, this meant Kelly, who I'd met up with fairly regularly, to discuss any problems she might be having and exchange ideas on the best strategies to deal with them. We'd also swapped numbers and email addresses so that we could be on hand in an emergency. It was yet another item on our ever-expanding job descriptions, but I didn't mind. It built relationships, and up to now it had worked well.

'Ah yes, of course you were,' Christine went on. 'I remember seeing it on your file, now I come to think about it. Even better then. Because it'll give you some context. The problem is the young lad they have in at the moment. The top and bottom of it is that they can no longer hold on to him, and we were wondering if you might be able to help out. Either for the short term until we find another long-term carer, obviously, or longer term, if that's something you'd want to think about.'

But I was thinking more about calm, capable Kelly. Both she and her husband seemed pretty good carers to me. 'Kelly can't take care of him?' I asked, surprised. She wasn't usually fazed by much. 'Why? And how old is he? What's his story?'

Christine laughed. 'You remember telling me about how your son can ask twenty questions in the same sentence? Well, now I know where he gets it from, don't I? Okay, well first of all you should know that had we not been thinking about you for that teenager that didn't materialise, we would have asked you to take on this one in the first place. He's a little lad called Sam Gough – he's nine, and has an unofficial diagnosis of autism. He was only removed from his mother just over a week ago – a single mum, mental health issues – along with his two siblings, who –'

'Just over a week ago? So Kelly's only had them for a matter of days?'

'Not them. Only Sam. His siblings have been fostered separately.'

This was highly unusual. 'Because?'

'Because they're very frightened of him, apparently. And yes, just the week. He has a number of issues. It could just be the shock of being taken from his family. Could be something completely different. But either way, he's been bullying Kelly and Steve's young children, and it's really impacting on the family.'

So, bad. Bad enough to be separated from his siblings, and bad enough that Kelly wanted him removed after only a week. Which was pretty bad. Pretty *challenging*. I eyed my sopping bikini. Reflected that aqua aerobics really wasn't for me. Not least because I already knew what my answer would be. However, protocol dictated that I think about it, and discuss it with my husband before agreeing, so I said what was expected of me and added, as an afterthought, 'as well as speaking to Mike, I'll finish dressing and nip into the canteen to give Kelly a quick call. It's always worth getting things from the horse's mouth, isn't it? Plus she'll be able to enlighten me on the day-to-day business of taking care of him.'

'Good idea,' Christine said. And I could tell by her jaunty tone that she knew she'd get her 'yes'. 'Oh, and one other thing,' she said. 'I know this will probably make you roll your eyes, but from the little I've heard about him, he does seem a perfect candidate for the type of programme you used to run – the behaviour modification thing that everyone was raving about a couple of years ago? Anyway, just a thought.'

A thought, or an extra inducement to be sure I didn't change my mind? If that was the case, then perhaps this little lad was even more challenging than I suspected. Because it was no secret that Christine, having hailed from Liverpool, where our particular programme hadn't been rolled out, had made it clear at the start of our working relationship that what *she* thought about the programme I thought so much of was that it was yet another new-fangled bit of nonsense that wouldn't bear fruit.

And she hadn't been the only one. In fact, the funding had been pulled after only four years. This was mostly due to tightening of government purse strings, but also – in my humble view – due to a lack of commitment to a philosophy the benefits of which might take a number of years to assess. So while it was true that fostering services were no longer training new carers in how to deliver the programme (and, as a consequence, children were no longer being hand-picked to receive it), those of us who had seen first-hand how effective it had been still used the model, and the principles, whenever we were fortunate enough to foster a child who looked like they might benefit. And here was Christine, the unbeliever, suggesting that Sam might be one such. She obviously needed to find a place for him, and fast.

Half an hour later, finally presentable, and having waved off my still-chuckling tormentors, I was sitting in a booth in the leisure-centre coffee shop, latte in one hand and mobile phone in the other, the not-so-sweet tang of chlorine still clinging to my hair.

'Oh, Casey, I feel soooo bad,' Kelly said, after I'd explained what the call was about. 'I had no idea it would be you they'd ring. You must think I'm such a wuss!'

'Don't be silly,' I reassured her. 'Honestly, we've all been through it. Sometimes you get a child in who just doesn't work in your particular environment. It happens. It's obviously not meant to be, so don't feel bad. I'm just ringing so that you can paint a clearer picture about what's been going on.'

'Just about everything,' Kelly said, before reeling off all of the problems she and Steve had faced in the last week. 'He's just such a live wire. I've never seen anything like it!'

Which seemed fair enough, because Kelly hadn't been fostering for very long. If she stuck at it – and I hoped she would – she would doubtless see worse. But it did sound pretty grim; in fact, to call Sam a 'live wire' seemed too benign a term, because as well as rampaging around her house, breaking and smashing things indiscriminately, he would apparently hurt her own children at every opportunity.

'Which I completely understand is all part of him expressing his rage,' Kelly said. 'But I can't take my eyes off him for a minute. And if I try to reason with him, or chastise him, he turns his anger on me instead. I know he's only small, but it's like being attacked by a whirling dervish. He really has no self-control, or self-soothing mechanism, at all. Well, perhaps one,' she added. 'This peculiar habit of barking and howling, which he does for prolonged periods at a time. And at any time he's confronted, he snarls. Really snarls. Poor Harvey said yesterday that it was like we had the big bad wolf living in the house.'

Harvey was Kelly's oldest. Around seven, as I remembered. And I wondered how it must feel to return home from school every day thinking there was a wolf living in your house. I wondered too how they'd come to ask Kelly, who was relatively inexperienced, to take on such a boy, knowing there were two younger children in the house. Not to mention that they already knew his own siblings were so afraid of him that it had been agreed to have them fostered somewhere else.

But that was a question for another day. And I probably already knew the answer: because there wasn't anyone else. Which Kelly must know too, so I imagined she'd feel pretty bad about passing the buck.

'So, how does the autism affect him?' I asked her instead. I'd looked after quite a few children who were on the spectrum and, in my experience, one size certainly didn't fit all. Each one of mine – and that included my own son, Kieron, who had Asperger's – had been very different, with different challenges to face.

'To be honest,' Kelly admitted, 'I haven't even really had the chance to notice. Everything else is so full-on, I just ... Oh, Jesus, hang on. Sam! Stop that right *now*!'

I waited on the line, listening to a symphony of different sounds – shouting and swearing and, at one point, high-pitched screaming. The jolly hold music of a call centre it definitely was not. No wonder her nerves were torn to shreds. Plus, it was Saturday now, of course, so both her kids would be home. And perhaps this had been the straw that had broken the camel's back.

'I'm so sorry, Casey,' she said as she came back to the phone, 'Sam's just bitten Harvey and now he's attacking Sienna. I honestly do not know what to do with him. It wouldn't be so bad if Steve was home but he's had to go into work this morning. And I'd take them out, but I – Sam! Right now! I *mean* it! – *God*, Casey. I am tearing my *hair* out here.'

I could tell she was, too, because she sounded on the verge of tears. 'Look, I can see it's a bad time,' I said. 'You obviously need to step in and get your own two to a place of safety. Shall I give you a call back later, perhaps when the kids are in bed?'

'*Call* me?' Kelly asked, her voice now even more desperate. 'I was rather hoping you'd come round and take him *off* me. As in *today*. Seriously. I know it's not the best endorsement you ever heard, but I can't take any more of this. I really can't.'

Knowing Kelly as I did, I knew she was telling me the truth. She was at breaking point, overwrought, and couldn't see a way out. It tended to be hard to with all your senses on high alert. No, it didn't sound so much, just having to oversee a naughty nine-year-old, but I knew there was 'naughty' and there was 'downright demolition-mode'; if she was dealing with the latter in isolation it would be a hard enough job – just in terms of trying to keep the child safe from himself. But with two little ones in the mix – her *own* little ones – it could be a Herculean task. And there was a world of difference between the odd flaring of temper and what sounded like twenty-four seven all-out warfare.

I knew the drill. I really shouldn't be making any promises. I should tell Kelly I'd speak to Mike and Christine and get back to her. But how could I? Besides, I was getting fired up now. No, I wouldn't be diving into any phone boxes, doing a spin and donning tights. But unlike my bikini top, I knew I had the strength for a challenge. And this lad sounded as if he was the word 'challenge' personified.

Plus, truth be told, I still had a few demons of my own to exorcise.

'Don't worry, love,' I told Kelly. 'I'll take him.'

Chapter 2

No matter how diverse the types of children who'd come to us over the years, my *modus operandi* for welcoming them rarely differed. In the here and now, one thing took priority over all others; to provide them with their own space – a place of comfort, calm and safety.

It had been a long time since we'd opened our home up to our first foster child, Justin, and as I went through my usual mental checklist for getting Sam's bedroom ready for his arrival, I reflected on just how much our singular job had become an everyday part of our lives. So much so that, these days, I was ready for every eventuality; stocked to the proverbial gunwales with everything I knew I'd need, or a frightened, disorientated child might want. Which meant that today it was a far cry from those anxious days before Justin was due to move in, when I'd run around like a mad thing, decorating, choosing, shopping and fussing over every detail, every imagined speck of dust.

Today, of course, I didn't have the luxury of time, but it didn't matter. It was really just a case of making up Sam's bed, and making everything nice for him. And as he'd bowled in from football training just an hour or so earlier, I also had Tyler, our long-term foster son, on hand.

Though we never thought of him as that, obviously, because 'son' pretty much covered it. He'd been with us seven years now. He was part of us for ever.

'Mum! Where d'you want this stuff?' he yelled from halfway down the loft ladder. From where I was smoothing the bedclothes all I could see were his legs and feet.

'In the conservatory!' I yelled back.

'What? Really?'

'Honestly, love, where do you *think* I'm going to want it?'

'Very funny. *Not*,' he said, staggering in carrying a giant beanbag, which he dumped, along with the brace of cushions I'd ask him to fetch down for me, right on top of the bed I'd just made up.

'Not on *there*,' I snapped. 'Now there'll be wrinkles in the duvet.'

'God, Mum,' he huffed. 'He's a nine-year-old, isn't he? You really think he's going to care if his duvet's a bit crumpled?'

'That's not the point,' I pointed out. 'It's a question of standards. Besides, *I'll* care. Anyway, thanks, love. Now go on down and tell your dad I'm almost finished, and that I'll be inspecting his dusting when I get there.'

I got the usual mock salute, accompanied by the usual grin and eye-roll, and as I always did when a new kid was about to be 'on the block', I thought back to the circumstances that had brought Ty himself to us – as angry and distressed a kid as you could ever wish to meet. A tightly wound ball of sheer fury, in fact, who'd greeted me (our first meeting had been at the police station where they were holding him) as if I'd been especially bussed in to torment him. A pint-sized harpy, sent to further ruin his already ruined day.

His ruined life, as it turned out. Well, or so it had seemed at that point. So to have got from that to this – to this lovely young man, who made us proud every day – still felt like a minor miracle. In fact, a series of miracles which, whenever times were tough, reminded me of that old, clichéd mantra – that unconditional love and firm boundaries could take you a very long way.

It had been less than eight hours since I had even heard the name Sam, and in around as many minutes I would be meeting him for the first time, too. Starting off on another journey into the unknown. And, as was fast becoming a norm now, with another almost completely unknown quantity; other than the concerns about his behaviour and the fact that he was in care, I knew almost nothing about this child. Because no one in social services did either.

I had a final check around. For all I knew, Sam could hate the Roblox-themed duvet cover I'd chosen. The blue curtains might offend him, and the fluffy yellow cushions I'd had Tyler bring down for him might, given he was unofficially diagnosed as autistic, make him cringe to the touch. And the books and games I had selected from my ever-growing storage boxes might be way out of his comprehension zone. I really was going in blind on this one – again! – and could only hope I'd hit one or two right notes. The rest I'd have to deal with as happened.

'Casey! Coffee ready, love!' Mike called up. 'Dusting done. Car pulling up. Come and join the welcoming committee.'

I closed the bedroom door and hurried anxiously downstairs. I always had butterflies in my stomach when about to meet a new child but today it was accompanied by another kind of anxiety. One that had been sparked when I'd called Kelly to tell her we were taking Sam and she had responded with such gratitude that it was almost embarrassing – as if I'd phoned her to tell her she'd won the lottery. She and her husband Steve had always seemed such capable, pragmatic carers, so I'd been surprised to hear so much emotion in her voice.

'I cannot thank you enough, Casey,' she'd gushed. 'I owe you. I owe you *big* time.'

'You owe me absolutely nothing,' I'd pointed out. And was just about to add that I was only doing my job when my internal censor (not always that reliable, to be honest) shut my mouth, because to do so would be to imply that she wasn't. At least I didn't doubt she'd have seen it that way.

Instead I burbled on about it being easier, since I didn't have little ones to think about, but when I rang off the intensity of her emotion still dogged me. Just how much of a challenge was this little boy going to be? Surely a child of nine couldn't be *that* much of a handful?

I said as much to Mike as he handed me my coffee and we prepared, as a family, to welcome our little visitor together – something that mattered at any time, obviously, but particularly with a child thought to be on the spectrum because change can be hard for such children. So to meet us as a single smiling unit – a wall of warmth and reassurance – would be helpful in managing his inevitable anxiety. Something now made much worse, of course, by this second, sudden, unexpected move and the confusion that would inevitably accompany it.

'Well,' Mike said, 'like you always say yourself, love, it doesn't matter where they come from, it only matters where they're going. You already knowing Kelly and Steve shouldn't really make a difference. And it sounds to me, given the situation with his own siblings, that it might not have been the best choice of family set-up.' He raised a palm. 'Though, yes, of *course* I know there probably wasn't a choice.'

'What will be, will be, I suppose,' I said, automatically checking that the kettle was filled enough to make Christine a cup of tea when she arrived. It was scalding. Mike had obviously beaten me to it, bless him.

And it was *only* to be Christine, which was highly unusual. A child would usually arrive with their social worker, too. But it turned out that Sam didn't even *have* a social worker. It had all happened so fast that the emergency duty team (EDT) had taken care of things, and apparently the only member of staff with space on his books – a Colin Sampson – was away on annual leave till the end of next week.

Colin would be assigned to Sam once he was back, at which point we'd all meet, but, in the meantime, if I had any sort of crisis I would have to call on the duty team. I mentally crossed my fingers that that wouldn't come to pass. Now I'd agreed to take him on, doing my best 'knightess on white charger' impression, I would look pretty stupid if I was calling out the cavalry within the week.

More to the point, the poor lad must be traumatised enough.

'Mum, I see him,' Tyler said from his station by the window. 'Aw, he's dead tiny, he looks really cute. Not sure what he's up to, exactly – he seems to be marching on the spot – but he definitely doesn't look dangerous.'

I'd given Tyler the facts, of course. It was important that he knew what we were dealing with. And following the problems our last foster child, Miller, had caused him, I couldn't blame him for checking Sam out. Things were okay now; on Miller's respite visits they rubbed along just fine. But every new child was a journey into the unknown for Tyler too.

And he was right. At first sight, Sam did indeed look very cute. Almost angelic, in fact, with shoulder-length, dirty-blond hair, which hung straight down over his skinny shoulders. And, as Tyler had observed, he seemed to be marching on the spot, while Christine stood by, patiently watching, holding a small suitcase. We all watched him too, till they finally set off down our front path, and I went to the front door to let them in.

Sam was shiny as a pin – Kelly had obviously bought a selection of new clothes for him – and like many a child before him, standing on this very spot, looked every bit as anxious as I'd expected.

'One hundred,' he announced, talking to a spot just above his feet. 'A one-hundred-step path. One hundred steps *exactly*.' He then wiped his brow theatrically, and exhaled as if he'd just climbed a very big hill. He straightened the backpack on his shoulders, and tugged on Christine's coat sleeve. 'That's a *very* long path, Mrs Bolton.'

Though I wasn't sure what to make of this, that was par for the course. But Christine gave me a quick glance before smiling at him and nodding. 'It certainly is, Sam, especially when we've had to do eighty-five of them on the spot. Sam has a bit of an obsession with the number one hundred, Casey,' she explained. 'It couldn't have been the number five or six, could it, Sam?'

I saw the trace of a smile cross the boy's elfin features. They'd obviously discussed this. And no doubt Christine would enlighten me later. In the meantime, it had broken the ice, and I laughed as I led them through to the dining area.

Mike was already setting down the teapot, Tyler pouring milk into a mug.

'Alright, mate?' he asked Sam. 'I'm Tyler. Pleased to meet you. Want a drink and a biscuit?'

Sam's gaze darted towards him, then away again. He shook his head.

'He's literally just had his tea,' Christine explained.

'Well, in that case,' Ty continued, as per our usual plan, 'do you want to come upstairs with me and see your bedroom?'

He held out a hand, and Sam eyed this too. Then, after checking wordlessly with Christine, who nodded an affirmative, began to shrug his backpack from his shoulders.

'Could you look after my bag, please?' he asked her politely. 'It's a Spider-Man backpack and it's very, very precious, so you won't let anyone near it, will you?'

'Absolutely not,' Christine assured him. 'Though why don't you take it with you? Find a safe place to put it in your new room?'

Sam stood and seemed to think, the bag gripped tightly in his tiny hands. He was extremely slight for nine. Malnourished? Possibly.

'Am I definitely, like, staying then?' he asked Christine, in a whisper.

'Yes, love,' she said gently. 'You're definitely staying. Remember? Like I told you? And I know you're going to like it.' She glanced at Tyler, then back at Sam. 'Go on,' she said. 'Go up with Tyler. See your bedroom, eh?'

'And mine too,' Tyler added, extending his hand a little further. 'I've got a PlayStation, and I might just have a Spider-Man game too.'

This seemed sufficient to seal the deal, and though the hand was ignored, Sam seemed happy enough – well, at least not *un*happy – to follow Tyler off upstairs.

'Damn,' I said to Christine, once they were safely out of earshot. 'Trust me to spurn Spider-Man for Roblox.'

'Oh, I really wouldn't worry. Kelly told me she only bought it for him a couple of days back. He didn't choose it. The counting to one hundred, though' – she nodded back towards the hallway – 'that's apparently quite a big thing with him. I have no idea why, or whether it has any significance, but apparently he does it all the time.'

Mike handed Christine her tea and we sat down around the table, so we could get all the paperwork done. Though in this case, there wasn't a lot of it. No history to peruse, obviously, just the usual Placement Plan. Plus a couple of signatures to confirm we took responsibility for any medical issues. And that was pretty much that – no more paperwork than you'd expect buying a second-hand car. Sold as seen. Sign on the dotted line and the child is all yours.

Christine must have read my thoughts. 'Here you go,' she said, smiling grimly as she handed me our copy. 'Far as I know, only one careful owner.'

Joking aside, this was a necessarily serious business. And as Christine began telling us what she did know, I had the usual sinking sense that I was being told an all-too familiar story.

The police had been called to the family home just over a week previously, after a neighbour had alerted them to screams and bangs coming from the house, and of furniture being thrown into the back garden. Upon arrival the police had quickly assessed the situation and, suspecting that the mother was under the influence of drugs, had called social services to attend.

'So, the two younger siblings were apparently found hiding underneath a bed,' Christine went on, 'whereas Sam was found in the back garden, shaking and terrified inside a big dog cage.'

'Ah, the barking and howling,' Mike commented.

Christine nodded. 'Exactly. In fact, if he hadn't been, they could easily have missed him altogether. And the mother was in such a state – a psychotic state, they realised – that a doctor was immediately summoned as well. When he arrived she was sedated and sectioned under the Mental Health Act and, of course, the children were all placed in care. And with different foster carers, as I mentioned to you this morning, Casey, on account of the other two being so terrified of poor Sam.'

Mike flicked his gaze towards the ceiling. 'As in *this* Sam? Who looks like he wouldn't say boo to a goose? You'd never think it, would you?'

We agreed we wouldn't. 'Any more on why?' I asked.

'Not really,' Christine said. 'Early days yet, and I'm sure we'll find out more, but one of the children apparently said he thought he was a dog. That he spent a lot of time living in the dog cage.'

'What *is* a dog cage when it's at home?' Mike asked.

'Well, like a kennel, I imagine,' Christine said.

'Or a crate, perhaps,' I suggested. 'You know, like in *Marley & Me*. Isn't crate-training a thing? I'm sure I've heard of it.'

'Probably,' Christine said. 'Though this one was definitely in the garden.'

'What about the dog?'

'No dog. They checked. No evidence of a pet either. They said it looked as though Sam spent a lot of time in there, though. It was decked out with blankets. Scraps of food. A few toys.'

'And they were genuinely that scared of him?'

'Apparently so.'

'But, even given that, it's still odd that their wishes were so readily taken on board, isn't it? Hard enough to find one foster family at such short notice, let alone two.'

'You're right,' she said, 'but I think the neighbour's comments were taken into account too. She told them Sam was practically feral – I know, you wouldn't credit it, would you? – and that she'd seen him attack his siblings on more than one occasion.'

I couldn't be shocked by what Christine was telling me because I'd heard him for myself when I was on the phone to Kelly. No, not the howling, but there was no question that he was out of control. But at the same time, could this really be the same boy? From what I'd seen with my own eyes, he'd seemed no more feral than I was. And I'd fostered near-feral children, so it wasn't as if I hadn't seen some.

Which meant nothing, of course; he'd been with Kelly for long enough to have been washed, scrubbed and polished. Except for one thing – it ramped up my compassion for the boy. It affected me deeply to think this little lad's brother and sister wanted to be away from him in a completely different home. It meant that not only did Sam have the trauma of going into care to deal with (away from his mother, and everything familiar – however grim life might sound for him, it was the only one he knew), but he also had the knowledge that even his siblings didn't want him. Enough to send anyone's behaviour spiralling out of control.

Christine didn't stay long. After a quick trip upstairs, to pop up Sam's suitcase and say goodbye, she left us, promising to let us know as and when she found out any more – though that would obviously be unlikely to happen before Monday morning. In the meantime, it was really just a case of watch and wait. Though in the shorter term, just a case of settling him in and putting him to bed, which, surprisingly, proved as simple a task as it sounded. It had been gone seven when they'd arrived, Sam had already eaten, and after the best part of an hour playing on the PlayStation with Tyler, it seemed that he didn't even need telling it was bedtime.

'Am I allowed to go to bed yet?' he asked when I checked on them.

'Yes, of course, love,' I told him. 'Shall I help you with your things?'

'I'm okay,' he said, getting to his feet, as Tyler paused

the game. 'I'm nine now,' he added. 'I can do stuff for myself.'

There was no side to him. No attitude. And he didn't seem to mind me watching as he trotted this room, unzipped his case and started rootling round for pyjamas. (That he'd have everything he needed wasn't going to be an issue, as I knew Kelly would have diligently packed everything she'd thought he might.)

'How about a glass of water?' I suggested, once he'd finally found them.

'I'm okay,' he said, briefly meeting my gaze. 'Night, night.'

My cue to go, then. So I did – only pointing out the bathroom, so he could clean his teeth. Which he did, albeit that I suspected this was a pretty recent ritual. I knew because I lingered with Tyler for a bit – duty done, he was getting ready to go out now – and heard Sam pad across to the bathroom minutes later. 'Seriously?' Tyler whispered to me. '*Feral*? If he's supposed to be feral, what does that make the eleven-year-old me?'

'Or the sixteen-year-old you, come to that,' I shot back at him.

But he was right. Could this be the same boy? Because when I peeked in on him later, just before heading to bed myself, he was sleeping, and looked the absolute picture of innocence. I wondered, as I pulled the door to, when this other child might show his face, the one that everyone was afraid of, with the devilish nature, the spiteful attitude, the belief that he was canine. Was that child really somewhere within Sam's cute, sweet, exterior?

But I'd been doing the job long enough to know appearances could be deceptive. That the answer was almost certainly 'yes'. And that, despite my observations, that child would probably show up soon enough. As sure as night followed day.

I switched off the landing light, and tiptoed across to my own bedroom. Fingers crossed not quite as soon as that, though.

Chapter 3

There is a place between sleep and waking which, if you linger there long enough, makes you forget where you are, where you've been and how you got there – which is why, for a few moments the next morning, I was knocked completely off guard by the strange sounds assaulting my ears.

Mike, too, it seemed. 'What the hell is that?' he spluttered, as he twisted around to check the time. 'God, it's not even bloody six o'clock!'

It was an animal sound, so my subconscious automatically supplied the details. 'Not those cats from next door, again,' I mumbled blearily. 'Honestly! You'd think she'd let them in in this weather.'

The noise continued, and, as it did so, I finally woke up properly, and realised that it was actually coming from inside our house. Which was when it hit me. Of *course*. We had a new child in. D'oh!

Comprehension having dawned, I sat up and shook

Mike's shoulder. 'Listen!' I said (as if he had a choice). 'I think it's Sam.'

Mike groaned, threw back the duvet and swung his legs out of bed. 'I think you're right, love. God, he's howling, isn't he? Just like they said. Better go and check on him.'

Gathering such senses as I could – early mornings, particularly in winter, were more Mike's domain than mine – I got up too, grabbed my dressing gown and pulled back the curtains. It was still fully dark. Just the street lamps were burning, illuminating the silvery sheen the frost had painted on the path. Which made the mournful sound coming from across the landing even more so. And very eerie. Like a werewolf in a movie.

Mike was already coming back in again as I was coming out. 'Very weird,' he said. 'It's almost like he's in some sort of trance. He's just lying there in his bed. Not moving or anything – just eyes shut and howling. No response when I spoke to him. Come on,' he beckoned. 'Come and look.'

I followed Mike into Sam's room, which was lit only by a night light, and where Sam, as Mike had said, was perfectly still in his bed. And I shuddered – were it not for the racket he was making, it was almost as if he was laid out at an undertaker's, before a funeral, his hair spread across the pillow and his hands clasped on his chest.

'Sam, love?' I whispered. 'It's Casey. You okay, sweetie?' Nothing. It was as if he didn't even realise we were there.

I touched his hand, and felt the heat of his soft, living skin. 'Sam, love?' But again, there was no response – just the merest hint of movement beneath his eyelids. But he didn't seemed at all agitated, and to intrude might distress him. Better, at least for now, to leave him to it, I decided.

I gently tugged on Mike's forearm and we shuffled back outside again. 'Let's leave him be for a bit,' I suggested. 'I think he's self-soothing. Probably his way of coping with waking up in yet another strange house.'

'What an odd way to go about it. Still, you're probably right. Let sleeping dogs lie, eh?' He mouthed 'boom-boom' in the half-light. 'Sorry. Couldn't help it. Anyway, I'd better go and shower. You okay to make the coffee? I need to get a shift on. We've a big delivery due in at seven.'

These days, Mike pretty much ran the warehouse where he worked, which meant long hours, sometimes even on a Sunday, like today, and greater responsibility. And with senior management having always been so understanding about our fostering – not least because it sometimes meant him taking time off at short notice – he took those responsibilities very seriously. It was a point of principle that he was never, ever late.

So I rattled down the stairs, got the coffee on and generally gathered myself together, all the while listening to an almost unbroken soundtrack of those unmistakeable rising and falling 'ah-oooo, ah-ooooooo' sounds.

Though not particularly loud or urgent, it was a sound that went through you, but, at the same time, if it soothed him, then I was loath to intervene. After all, I reasoned, it would defeat the whole purpose if he wasn't allowed to do what made him feel better. Even so, I gave myself a mental time limit. Once Mike had gone to work, I would go up again and see if I could rouse him.

Mike having left to do just that, I was just about to head up and do so when a very confused-looking Tyler appeared in the kitchen.

'What's going on up there?' he asked, sleepily rubbing his eyes. 'Have you been in and seen him? What on earth is he doing?'

'Howling, love,' I said as I finished off my coffee (and reflected that 'howling, love' was such an unlikely thing to find yourself saying if you weren't in a horror film). 'Apparently, he used to act like a dog to scare his younger brother and sister. But I think it's more that *he's* scared. And that he's howling to soothe himself. We once looked after another little boy who had autism, and he used to flap his arms, a bit like a bird, when he was stressed or afraid of a situation.'

'Sam's autistic?' Tyler asked. 'Really? He doesn't seem autistic.'

'It's a very broad spectrum, love,' I explained. 'Some signs are hardly noticeable and others a lot more so. Sam hasn't been officially diagnosed but he must have displayed some of the signs for it to be mentioned in his file, but we'll just have to wait and see. You never know, this howling might be the extent of it.'

Tyler shuffled across the kitchen to grab a box of cereal. As was often the case, now he'd started at college, he had a full schedule of Sunday-morning football to attend, and needed a suitably hearty breakfast. Though possibly a little earlier than he'd planned.

'Shall I cook you something love?' I said.

He shook his head. 'Don't worry, Mum. I'll see to it. You want me to make a bacon sarnie for you too? You need to deal with – ah. Hold up. I think he's stopped finally.'

I listened. 'Yes, you're right. I think he has. I'll nip up and see what's happening. Oh, and double yes about that sandwich, with brown sauce and knobs on. Because I suspect this might just be the calm before the storm.'

I hurried back upstairs. 'Morning, sweetie!' I called out brightly after knocking and entering. 'Would you like to come downstairs and have some breakfast with me and Tyler? I'll pop some cartoons on for you while we get things ready, if you like.'

Sam was still lying on his back, staring blankly at the ceiling. But he was aware of my presence now, because he immediately turned to look at me. He looked confused at first – not surprisingly – but then smiled and sat up, and swung his legs out of the bed.

It was an odd smile, however, that didn't quite seem to reach his eyes, and I tried to remember where I'd seen that before. It hit me then that it had been Georgie, the autistic boy I'd just mentioned to Tyler. When I spoke to him, he'd often adopt that exact expression – as if he knew what a smile was, but didn't really feel it. Just understood, or had been taught, when he was expected to produce one.

'I like cartoons,' Sam said. Then he pointed at his pyjamas, 'Look, Mrs Bolton,' he said. 'See? These are cartoon pyjamas. Fireman Sam. The lady got them for me because I'm a Sam too. And *I'm* going be a fireman as well.'

I laughed and held out my hand. 'Come on then, Fireman Sam. And Mrs Bolton – Christine – is the lady who brought you yesterday. My name is Casey, remember?'

Sam took my hand, which surprised me, and nodded. 'Choo, choo! Casey Jones!' he said, pulling on an invisible train whistle with his other hand. And this time his accompanying smile seemed more genuine. 'I know that story, too. You know, you should be a train driver.'

I smiled back. This kid was certainly full of surprises. How on earth did he know about a TV show that pre-dated even me?

'You know what?' I said, as we walked, companionably hand-in-hand, down the stairs. 'I would have loved to be a train driver. But I couldn't get a job. I was too short to see over the engine.'

'For real?' he said, eyes wide.

'Just kidding,' I told him. 'So. What would you like for breakfast? Cereal? Bacon sandwich? Boiled eggs and soldiers?'

'Boiled eggs and *soldiers*?'

'You mean you've never eaten soldiers?'

Sam shook his head. He looked flummoxed. 'What, *real* soldiers?'

A Dark Secret

'Yes, absolutely. But made of bread, so you can stick them in the egg. If you listen closely, you can hear them going "oi!"'

I studied Sam while Tyler and I made short work of our bacon sandwiches, and our little visitor wolfed down his eggs and soldiers. What a complicated little lad he was. And an immature one, as well – both physically and mentally. Though not immature in the pejorative sense of the word. I was just building a picture of a boy half his age. The precious backpack, the pyjamas and the talk of being a fireman – a fine ambition at any age, of course, but, in tandem with what I knew of his regular toddler-tantrum-like outbursts, I felt sure I was in the presence of arrested development, of a child who had probably missed many milestones. And conceivably, given the little I did know of his background, a fair bit of schooling. Possibly as a result of his autism or neglect, and perhaps both; a child who'd never heard of boiled eggs and soldiers.

But Sam had definitely heard of Lego. And once Tyler had left, and I got my enormous crate of bricks out, he fell upon it as if I'd handed him the keys to the proverbial sweetshop, having never in his life, he told me, wide-eyed and breathless, seen so much of it, in one place, all at once.

Let alone been allowed to play with it. So Lego it was, then, and since he didn't want me to help him, I switched the telly to a daytime chat show (a rare, guilty pleasure), happy to just observe as he tipped the entire box onto the carpet and, once he'd gathered up and sorted what he needed into neat different-coloured piles, set about making 'the biggest, bestest bridge ever'.

And after an hour during which he was completely absorbed, he had indeed built something pretty magnificent. Whatever problems there might be with his emotional and social development, his engineering skills, eye for detail and spatial awareness really were something to behold.

And I was just about to say so when the whole thing went pear-shaped, and the much-heralded wild child, who rampaged like an animal, showed up to join us, as if from nowhere.

And it really was out of nowhere. I'd had absolutely no inkling. One minute he was sitting back on his heels admiring what he'd made – I had shuffled forwards on the sofa and muted the telly so I could inspect it too – and the next he was on his feet and, completely without warning, had karate-kicked a foot out to smash it to pieces – a full-on sideways thrust right at the middle of it with his bare foot.

'I hate you!' he screamed at it. 'I *hate* you! I *hate* you!' And once he'd reduced it to a pile of bricks again, he kicked at it some more, sending showers of bricks pinging all across the room.

'Sam! What on earth's wrong?' I asked. 'Why on *earth* have you done that? Your bridge was brilliant. Why would you smash it into pieces like that?'

He whirled to face me. 'Cos it's shit!' he screamed, stabbing a finger towards the mess he'd made. 'The colours got all wrong! This Lego is shit! I don't want it! I hate it!'

'The colours got wrong?' I asked, keeping my voice low to try and calm things. 'What d'you mean, love? The colours looked lovely to me.'

I should have known better than to disagree with him, because this only made him crosser. 'The colours got *wrong*!' he raged. Then, again without warning, he lunged at me, grabbed my hair and began pulling.

What a sight we must have looked to anyone passing by – me still perched on the sofa, Sam's face at my eye level, pink-cheeked with fury, two clumps of my hair clutched tight in his fists. I could feel his warm breath puffing in angry gusts on my face.

'I hate you! I hate you!' he screamed, pulling harder, now kicking out with his feet at my shins as well. Thanking God for him being shoeless, I unfolded myself to standing, though with my head dipped, of necessity, to the level of his chest.

'Sam, let go of my hair, please,' I said through a veil of it.

In answer, he tugged harder. I put my hands over his. 'Sam. Let go of my hair, please. *Now.*'

Another tug, this time accessorised by an eardrum-splitting scream. 'Sam!' I shouted, now forcibly unbending his fingers. 'You need to listen to me. Let go this minute. Calm down!'

He was screaming at such a pitch now that I doubted he could even hear me. But my greater strength won out and I managed to free my hair. His own hands I hung on to though, tightly. What must this kind of assault be like if you were the same size as he was? Or smaller – Kelly's fears for her poor kids were now making sense. And no wonder his own siblings were so scared of him.

'Sam! *Listen* to me,' I said firmly, holding his hands now in front of him. 'I want to help you. I want to help you figure out what went wrong with your bridge. But I cannot do that – I cannot *help* you – while you're this angry.'

His eyes were full of tears now. 'It was the blues! It was the blues!'

I saw his leg twitch, and braced for another kick, but it didn't come. I lowered my backside back onto the sofa so we were again face-to-face. 'Okay, so that's a start,' I said. 'Sam, look at me. *Look* at me. There. That's a start. So, what about the blues? What exactly went wrong with them?'

'There was a *wrong* one!' His tone suggested he was incredulous that I could have missed it. 'A blue one where there shouldn't have been one! And I never did it! I did a red, then a white, then a blue, then a red again. But I never put two blues together. I never!'

Wow, I thought, *he has misplaced a brick. That is all*. 'Ah, I see,' I said. 'Well, yes, I can see how that would make you cross. So perhaps it's best if we put the bricks away for today, okay? So here's what we're going to do. We're going to pick them all up, *together*, and put them back in the box. Then how about I see if I can find *Fireman Sam* on the telly?'

'But *I* never *did* it!' he squeaked at me. 'I *never*!'

But I could tell from his changing body language that this was only the embers. The raging fire, quick to ignite, had died away equally quickly. I let go of his hands finally. He flexed and unflexed his fingers.

'Come on,' I said, getting down on my knees now. 'Tell you what, shall we make it a race?'

In answer, he was down on his own knees in seconds, gathering. 'Beat ya, beat ya, beat ya!' he sang. 'Gotcha, gonna eat ya!'

Which made little sense to me, but that was absolutely fine. The important thing was that the storm had passed as quickly as it had started. And at least we'd had it, which meant that we were at last up and running. And though I didn't know to where, quite, with this tornado of a child, at least I had a better idea of what I was dealing with.

Chapter 4

If that one small incident opened a window to what Kelly might have been dealing with, the next couple of days saw me thrown headlong straight out of it, and onto what I had to concede was something fast approaching a battlefield. Life with Sam was definitely going to be no picnic. No wonder Kelly, with two little ones, had struggled to cope. Because it wasn't just the screaming and the howling and the tantrums, and it wasn't just the constant threat of violence when Sam exploded. It was that I just never saw them coming.

And they seemed destined to be a regular occurrence. That same afternoon, after Mike and Tyler had returned, I was in the kitchen, toiling away at a late-afternoon roast, when there was another major blow-up.

Sam had been watching TV while Mike and Tyler had been going over some college coursework, and, as the volume had been creeping up to a disruptive level, Mike had asked Sam if he could turn it down a little. He'd duly nodded – this was apparently no problem in itself, because he did as he was told immediately – but when he accidentally pressed the 'change channel' button, and lost the programme temporarily, it triggered a second bout of screaming and swearing and lashing out – this time, and just as I ran into the living room, by throwing the remote across the room in a fit of temper, catching Tyler a glancing blow across the face.

Mike was obviously quick to act, grabbing Sam up in a bear hug before he could lay hands on anything else to throw, and while Tyler heroically took the blow – in both senses – on the chin, Mike was already deploying the restraint technique we'd been trained in; using his superior strength to physically contain Sam while trying to quell the storm of his temper.

And what a whirlwind of a thing that temper was. Mike had his arms firmly around Sam, pinning his own to his sides, but I could see he was looking for any opportunity to attack, gnashing his teeth, and trying to get his mouth close enough to bite Mike, while kicking his feet out to try and kick him on the shins. Had he not been just nine – and such a scrap of a thing – it would have been a fearsome sight. As it was it just made me feel very sad.

While Tyler gathered up the batteries and put the remote back together, I went across to see if I could help. 'Sam, until you stop that silly kicking and biting, Mike can't let you go,' I tried. 'The way you are carrying on, you will hurt yourself, and we don't want that to happen.

We just want you to calm yourself down, okay? So stop yelling and take some deep breaths, please.'

But the only thing Sam was listening to was his anger, which seemed to be drowning all other sounds out. Eyes squeezed tight shut, he continued to wriggle and squirm. 'Are you listening, mate?' Mike asked. 'You need to stop this, okay? Because I can't let you go till you do.'

Mike shuffled back a little, towards the sofa, pulling Sam up onto his lap, speaking softly as he did so despite the heels hammering at his shins. 'There we go, mate,' he said, as he cradled and rocked him. 'That's better, you're settling down now. Come on, shhhh, stop your fuss now, that's it, in and out, take deep breaths.'

And, bit by bit, once again, the storm began to ebb away. Whether by will or exhaustion, I had no idea, but after ten minutes it appeared to have passed altogether, and once he was limp in Mike's arms, his eyes finally open, I took a chance – those little feet could pack one heck of a punch – and knelt down in front of him on the carpet.

'Sam, d'you want to talk?' I asked. 'About what made you angry?'

His eyes flicked past me to where Tyler was standing, holding the remote.

'Stupid buttons!' he said immediately. 'The stupid buttons make me angry. They're *rubbish* buttons,' he added. 'They're just *stupid*.'

'They're just buttons, love,' I pointed out. 'Are they really worth getting in such a pickle about? Tell you what, how about Tyler sits down with you after dinner, and goes through what all the different buttons do with you? Would that help, do you think? Though for now, I think you first need to say sorry to him, don't you?'

'Mum, it's fine,' Tyler began. 'He didn't mean –'

'Exactly. I didn't *mean* to,' Sam finished for him.

'Nevertheless,' I said, 'it hit him, and you were the one who threw it. Which makes it a consequence of an action *you* took, Sam. Which is something I'd like you to think about, okay? And meanwhile, I'd better get back to the kitchen, or none of us will be getting any tea tonight, will we?'

Sam's chin jutted as he looked at me, apparently astonished. 'I'm *allowed* tea?'

'Of course you are, mate,' Mike said. He too took a chance and let his arms fall away. 'Can't have a little scrap like you starving, can we?'

Sam twisted round to look at him. 'Even though I'm bad? I still get *tea*?'

I touched Sam gently on his head. His forehead was damp from his exertions, as was his hair. 'Of course you get tea, silly. And you're not bad, love,' I said. 'You're just a little boy who gets angry quite a lot, and we're going to all have to work together to help you with that. And we will. Though in the meantime' – I got to my feet and put my hand out – 'how about you come into the kitchen and help me with the veg, so Mike and Tyler can finish off what they're doing?'

Sam managed a smile as he took my hand. 'Are we having peas?' he asked. 'I could count them. I'm good at counting peas.'

I think we all chuckled in unison. 'I'm not sure we actually *need* to count them,' I told him. 'But yes, if you want
peas, we can definitely have peas. But first, are you going
to say sorry to Tyler?'

'Oh, yeah, sorry,' he said. Then trotted off with me,
happy as Larry. What a conundrum this little boy was.

I pondered the puzzle of Sam as I finished preparing
dinner and, deprived of counting peas, he helped sort out
the cutlery instead. Because it *was* a puzzle. There being
no unhappy aftermath to Sam's violent outbursts – at least
so far – was interesting in itself. As had been the case
earlier in the day, once Sam was over his anger, it was as
if he'd forgotten all about it. No contrition. No regret.
But no sullen defiance either. Though he'd been genuinely astonished that he was still going to be fed after what
he'd done (which meant he definitely understood we had
issues about his behaviour), his own 'moral compass' – his
personal landscape of what was and wasn't acceptable –
seemed oddly absent. Whereas most kids, even the most
damaged, out-of-control kids, had an understanding that
their behaviour negatively impacted on others (more
often than not, that was precisely why they did it), it
almost seemed as if Sam rationalised them on a 'what's
done is done' basis. Since he had no problem brushing
them off once they were over – and forgetting them
completely – it didn't seem to occur to him that we
wouldn't too. I was no psychologist, but I found Sam's
psychology fascinating. It was as if he was living in the

moment, but to the nth degree. So much so that it was as if his previous rages hadn't even happened.

Yet, happen they had, and happen they did again. And, over the next twenty-four hours, they happened at regular intervals. Without warning, the slightest thing could tip him over into a raging, yelling bundle of fury. Because the eggs and soldiers hadn't been set out the same way as yesterday. Because he'd coloured over the lines in the colouring-in book I'd given him. Because someone on *Fireman Sam* didn't do what Sam thought he should do. By the time Monday evening came around, I looked as if I'd done a few rounds myself – in a boxing ring with Anthony Joshua.

'We can't allow this to continue,' Mike said once we'd put Sam to bed that evening, after another flare-up over some nonsense or other. Yet another episode during which I'd had a fistful of hair grabbed.

'I know,' I said. 'I'd be tearing my own hair out, but he's busy doing it for me. I'll be flipping bald soon, at this rate!' I felt my scalp, which was so tender that I winced as I touched it. 'I just wish I could get a handle on his triggers.'

'Sure you're not just clutching at straws?' Mike said. 'Because from what I've seen and you've described, anything could be a trigger. He's just in max on-the-edge mode, twenty-four seven. How can we get to the bottom of something we can't see coming?'

Yet, for all that Mike was right (he had to be – how else to explain the rages?) when he wasn't flying off the handle

Sam was no trouble at all. Quite the opposite, in fact. Though I'd been anxious that Tyler would lose his rag sooner or later, when I'd gently probed him about Sam (he was now out for the evening) he'd laughed it all off, apparently genuinely.

'It's obviously going to be like living with a little cyclone,' he'd admitted. 'But as long as he doesn't touch my stuff I can live with it.'

'Seriously?' I'd asked. After the troubles we'd had with Miller, I was anxious above anything that we didn't have a re-run. Happy as I was to take on Sam, it just wouldn't be fair.

'Seriously,' he'd reassured me. 'I know it's going to sound weird, Mum, but I quite like him. He's sweet.'

And though I knew Mike wasn't convinced yet, what Tyler had said had struck a chord with me. Bottom line was that I liked Sam too. Which was no way a requisite for caring for him and doing my best for him, but it was a happy extra fact. And a welcome one, too. Whatever else it was, it was a plus point, because we were at the start of a journey that could end up as rocky as many others I'd already taken. A little stock of goodwill and sympathy would be a big bonus.

'You're right,' I agreed with Mike now, 'but, you know, even only forty-eight hours in, I feel we're already gathering pieces of the jigsaw. His comment about being fed when he'd been "bad" – that was telling, for instance. No, I know it's not earth-shattering knowing he was probably punished by being denied food, but it's something, isn't it?

Not a lot, but something. And all the kicking, biting, hair-pulling – that doesn't just come from nowhere. It's learned behaviour. As is all the dog stuff. I think I need to do some comprehensive note-taking with this one, because although it all seems kind of random in the moment, we might just find a pattern if we record everything.'

I could see from Mike's expression that he knew I was on a roll. But I could also see that he wasn't yet rolling with me. 'Well okay, love, I guess you know what you're doing, but it's one thing him attacking us and Ty, but what about when the grandkids come round? Have you thought about that?'

'Of course I have,' I sniffed. 'I can't believe you've even asked that. In fact, I filled Riley and Kieron in this afternoon, before you got home. And, yes, I've pre-warned them that things might be a little sticky in the short term, but it's not like we're going to have them round here and leave them alone with him unsupervised. And, besides, Levi and Jackson are both older than Sam – and stronger, don't forget. I doubt he'd give them any nonsense. I doubt he'd dare. And as for the girls –'

'Case, there you go. That's *exactly* what I'm getting at. It's all well and good dealing with it after the fact, but in the meantime one of the kids might have been frightened or even hurt, and we can't ask them not to come to the house, can we? I just think we need to be clear that Sam poses a risk to them, and be upfront about how – and if – we want to manage that. I don't think either of us want a re-run of Miller. No, I know we don't, in fact.'

I didn't like the turn this conversation was taking. Not one bit. 'So you're saying we shouldn't commit to Sam yet?'

'No, I'm not saying that. I'm just saying – and don't throw a cushion at me, okay? – that we should be clear that if Sam continues with these violent outbursts there is a line to be drawn, and we're not going to cross it. That our grandkids being safe here with *any* foster kid is non-negotiable. One thing you being covered in bruises, because you're tough as nails, you are, but quite another it happening to them. Isn't that fair?' He looked at me pointedly.

Which he had a right to. I'd bent his ear enough about Miller, after all. He knew more than anyone just how close I'd come to throwing in the fostering towel with him. So perhaps he was just pre-empting things; looking out for me.

But I was gung-ho. I don't know why, but I just felt I could get a handle on Sam – get through to him, autism or no autism. 'Oh, stop looking for problems that may not exist, love.' I grinned at him. 'You know I hate when you do that.'

Mike laughed. 'No, love, what you hate is when I touch on your *own* fears. You know as well as I do that this could be a real issue.'

As I went to put the kettle on I felt an overwhelming urge to let out a growl myself, because what I hated even more than that was admitting that Mike was right, and I *might* be wrong.

So I'd just have to prove him wrong, wouldn't I?

Chapter 5

It felt a little like saying hello to an old friend. Not in reality; all the previous examples in my life had long gone now, along with the children with whom I'd made them. But in gathering what I'd need to make a chart for Sam – the stickers, the paper, the array of felt pens – I felt the warm glow of re-acquaintance with a cherished buddy.

When was the last time I'd set about my job with my old friend to support me? Too long, it seemed to me. Much too long. If I'd been slightly stung by Christine's opinion of our points system when I'd first met her, now I was even more zealous. And because it had been her suggestion that we try helping Sam within its framework, I also felt vindicated – which made me even more determined to prove the naysayers wrong. For some children, in some circumstances, positive and structured behaviour modification was the key to unlock the potential for better lives.

That we needed to access that key in Sam was increasingly obvious. We knew almost nothing about him yet, and I doubted we would for a few days more, but whatever the underlying issues for his various behaviours, helping him to find ways to quash them before they completely took hold of him would be essential if we were to try and help him come to terms with his situation and his past.

Whatever that past might turn out to be. We were three days in now and still I knew nothing of his history. He'd offered nothing either, and I'd decided not to press. Instead, after another day spent mostly fire-fighting his tantrums, I had made copious notes, both in my head and in my journal. And having assembled all my equipment, I now sat and read through the latter, marking the ones which I felt we should prioritise; not just the obvious issue of him lashing out in anger (obviously the main one) but also personal care, household chores and an array of social niceties that, when implemented, would add that positive bit of structure to his days.

It wasn't as simple a business as might be expected, however. With children like Sam, a list of 'don't dos' and 'you must dos' would be useless. The most effective way to deal with undesirable behaviours (such as anger, quick temper or being fast-reactive) was to put tasks into place that he could readily do but required patience, thought and determination. It would be a slow process – as with Rome, desired behaviours really weren't built in a day – but the ongoing sense of achievement, built in lots of small ways, would hopefully see those negative behaviours begin subsiding.

But first Sam needed concrete incentives. If he didn't understand that he was doing anything wrong, then, without being offered something in return, why would he change? Again, this wouldn't necessarily be a simple thing to achieve, because the usual trade of 'do this and you'll get that' generally didn't work well with children at Sam's intellectual/emotional level. So it was more about giving him control. If we established the things he wanted, and gave him options for ways to get them, then he could choose to work towards them. If he wanted a takeaway pizza at the weekend, he could be proactive in trying to earn one – choosing to do the tasks necessary for him to be rewarded.

Or not. Though the 'not' bit wasn't part of the plan. Not initially. Nor were his undesirable behaviours. Where more emotionally robust children could cope with losing points as well as earning them, and, as a consequence, try harder after precious 'ticks' had been lost, other children – the most vulnerable – would react very differently; one 'failure' would immediately send them into a spin, thinking (because negative thinking can be such an ingrained behaviour) that they had failed, period, and that all was now lost. And this in itself would lead to more 'bad' behaviour.

So it was all about keeping things positive – if Sam didn't feel like doing a chore, or was too busy acting up to finish one, he could simply regroup and try again for it the next day.

And, having had the green light from Christine, even before I'd met him, I'd prepared for Sam's arrival with this kind of behaviour modification already in mind. Which was why, before he got to us, I had already done some of the work necessary to put my plans into action; the bedroom he'd been given was already free of the two things that (sad to say, some would say, but this was the real world, in *this* world) I knew could be used as inducements, namely the small television that habitually resided there and, usually attached to it, Kieron's old Xbox. Given what I'd observed in the days Sam had been with us, these two items would, I knew, provide incentives.

But now the real work began. After a third morning in which Sam had howled in bed for half an hour, I'd brought him down for breakfast (Mike and Tyler having gone to work and college) and, once we'd eaten, had allowed him to watch TV in the living room while I gathered my equipment on the dining table.

Now I drained my coffee and suggested he might like to come and join me, to play a game I thought he might enjoy.

'It's a special game,' I told him, as I pulled a dining chair out for him to sit on. 'One where the idea is to make life a bit easier for you.'

He sat as instructed and eyed all the paper and pens. 'Are we doing colouring in?' he asked. 'Shall I draw you a fire engine?'

'Not yet,' I said, 'but we can after this, if you like. No, what I thought we could do first of all is find out what things you would really like.' I picked up my pen. 'And when you tell me, I can make a list of them.'

Sam's hand shot up immediately, just as it might in a classroom. 'A dog,' he enthused. 'I really, really want a dog.'

My heart sank just a little. Not the best of starts, obviously. Since having our first foster child, Justin – when Bob, our dog, had been at risk of serious harm – having a pet in the house had become a no-no. So Bob (now in doggy heaven) had gone to live his life out with Kieron. But Kieron now had another dog, a little Westie called Luna. 'Not a dog, sweetie. We can't have a dog here, I'm afraid. But shall I tell you something? My son Kieron has a dog. If you'd like to we could certainly go and visit him.'

'A big dog or a little dog?' he asked. I filed the question away.

'A little dog.'

'Good,' he said. 'I like little dogs the best.'

I filed that one away too. But chanced a supplementary question.

'Did you used to have a dog?' I asked.

'*No*,' he said immediately. A little too immediately. 'I never.'

'You'd just like one.'

'Really, really,' he said.

'Well, as I say, we can't have one here, but if you like little dogs, you'll definitely like Luna. And hopefully you'll get to meet her soon. So, think again. What else?'

'Um …' he said, 'um …', his brow furrowed in concentration.

'How about I suggest something?' I offered, pretending to think hard, as he had. 'How about a TV in your bedroom?'

His eyes became like saucers. 'Oh my *God*, yes!' he said. 'Could I *really*? That would be *way* cool.'

I wrote 'television' down on one of my pieces of paper. 'Okay,' I said. 'Then how about, say, an hour to play on my laptop?'

'Your laptop? Your actual laptop?'

'My actual laptop. And, let me see now, maybe something like an Xbox in your room?'

Sam jumped from his chair at this, and punched the air, twice. 'It's like Christmas for good kids!' he shouted. 'Yes, yes!'

'Hang on,' I said, laughing. 'We're not finished yet. What other things would you most like?'

'I like *everything*,' he said, sitting down again.

'So, if I add a trip to the cinema, a new toy, a takeaway … and how about a movie night? Curtains shut, so it's like the cinema, and with popcorn and everything.' I glanced up from my scribbling. 'Those things sound alright to you?'

But Sam had stopped laughing suddenly, and was staring at my list now. I didn't know why, or what I'd said, but something had definitely just happened to create a change.

I touched his arm. 'What d'you think, love?'

He turned his gaze to me. 'What do I have to do?' he asked, his voice now low and quiet. 'Do I have to count to lots of one hundreds?'

Again, I filed his words away to ponder over later. But in the meantime I was at least pleased to notice that he was beginning to understand there had to be a trade-off. 'No, silly,' I said, smiling. 'No counting needed. But, yes, you are right in that to get things you first have to earn them. I'm sure you've learned all about that in school?'

He shrugged his shoulders. 'I s'pose,' he said, but his enthusiasm was definitely on the wane now.

I reached for a second sheet of paper. 'So,' I said, 'now we have to make another list. Of how you could get to have all those things. But, come on, you help me – what do *you* think you could do?'

He was still looking at me with that odd, anxious expression, and I feared that the whole process might be derailed any moment – that he'd lose his rag, declare things 'rubbish' and generally kick off.

But he didn't do anything. He just sat there looking sad. 'I don't think I want to do anything,' he said eventually. Then he thought for a moment. 'Or, maybe, I could run to the shops for you?'

It had come out of leftfield, creating a vivid image. Of little Sam hurrying down the street carrying a list and a Tesco bag for life. Such a simple thing to do, in a happy, secure childhood. And it touched me. Made me feel sad too.

It was also a discussion for another day – one down the line a bit. He was nine and an unknown quantity, so it was also a safeguarding issue. 'No, nothing like that,' I said, 'though it's a lovely idea, Sam. No, let me think. I was thinking more of things round the house. Like, how about, I know … making your bed every morning?'

He nodded. 'Then maybe being quiet in your room until you hear an adult get up, perhaps? Brushing your teeth twice a day? Taking out the rubbish bags to the bins?'

I was writing as I spoke and I could see Sam eyeing the list, and I could tell by his expression – which was approaching incredulous – that he thought this was far too easy a trade.

It also seemed to cheer him up from whatever had upset him. 'I could do all of that,' he said. 'Easy. And I could wash up, and dry up, and help put the pots away,' – now we're rolling, I thought – 'and I'm good at digging. I can dig the garden up for you if you like.'

I had another vision – of my flower beds, and how well they might fare under his enthusiastic ministrations. 'Well, I think we'll leave the garden till it's properly springtime,' I told him. 'But if you're happy with all the others, I think that would be brilliant. So,' I said, sitting back a little, 'now we have what we need to play the game. The list of things you'd like, and the list of things you can do to help you get them. So now we come to this chart –' Like a *Blue Peter* presenter, I reached for the one I'd prepared earlier.

'What's that?' he said, his interest piqued. 'What's the lines for?'

'These are rows and columns,' I explained as we pored over it together. 'We put the tasks down on this side, and the days of the week up here, and every time you complete one, we mark it with a tick. Well, not a tick, but a star' – I reached for them – 'like this. Then we count up all the stars and check the list of treats, and you can chose those you've earned enough stars for. Then we do exactly the same the next week, and the next week, and the next week. Maybe change the treats, if you decide there are other things you'd like to earn. But that's pretty much how it works. Does that make sense?'

'I'm not sure. I *think* so.'

'Don't worry. It will make more sense when we've filled in all the boxes. Shall we do that now?'

'Yes, yes,' he enthused, 'so I can start straight away. Easy peasy!'

It wasn't quite as simple as that, obviously, because nothing worthwhile ever is. And, down the line – well, assuming all went roughly to plan – it would, of necessity, become more complicated. He could only 'earn' the TV and Xbox once, obviously, so at some point he'd have to understand that, in order just to keep them, certain tasks would need completing regularly. Which could create another crisis (it had done so with Justin) and that would need to be managed too, when it came to it – but it was important that we did, because it was another important step on the road to a child taking ownership of their own behaviour.

But that was for later. For the moment it was sufficient that we were sitting companionably at the table, and that Sam was embarking, willingly, on the all-important first step – engaging with a process that could reap huge rewards for him, and which would occupying him productively and, hopefully, as a by-product, help his more negative behaviours to melt away a bit.

At least, that was the theory …

Chapter 6

By the middle of the second week – i.e. the one after the weekend we'd pencilled in that precious mini-break – I was busy pencilling ticks in my head. Not actual ticks – the 'ticking' took the shape of coloured stars stuck on Sam's chart – but little 'pride' ticks because, despite my realistically low expectations, Sam had surprised both me and Mike by proving us wrong. Because the chart seemed to be working, at least after a fashion. Yes, he was still at times the sort of child that inspired pipe dreams of that precious mini-break, but there was no denying that every morning I had a 'sort of' made-up bed, that Sam 'sort of' brushed his teeth and that, most days, at least, he seemed genuinely eager to get all his 'very important' jobs done. Yes, his overly zealous contribution to washing the pots meant that I had already lost one milk jug, one cereal bowl and two mugs, but I figured that, compared to the havoc he'd already wreaked, a few items of old crockery were acceptable collateral.

And, contrary to his previous attitude to breakages (mostly 'stuff them'), he had begun to care about the consequences of destroying things. 'I don't get struck off, do I?' he'd asked anxiously the first time he smashed something.

'Struck off?' I asked, wondering at the curious turn of phrase. 'No, sweetie, once you get your star, you *keep* your star,' I told him. 'We've been over this, remember? And you're doing a *great* job. Just try to go a little slower and you'll be fine.'

And he'd take it on board, and he'd try to be careful, and for periods during the day it was possible to forget that this was a child with a whole host of challenges to face; one to which a 'one step forward, two steps back' mantra still very much applied. That we might just be in a honeymoon period.

Because he was also, in this new incarnation, extremely endearing – as if he'd been bussed in especially, to become the poster-boy for the points programme. Which he took extremely seriously, and in unexpected ways, such as his approach to the business of staying quiet in his room till an adult was up and about.

Because, to my surprise, the early morning howling had ceased right away. Which obviously made me question the purpose of the behaviour. Perhaps it hadn't been a self-soothing mechanism, after all. Perhaps it was more akin to the sort of 'happy babbling' Kieron used to do in his cot when he was a baby.

It was only by chance, a few days in, that I learned

differently. I'd risen early – before Mike – fancying a long, leisurely bath, before those with places to be hogged the bathroom. And was just crossing the landing when I heard a low, slightly worrying, gurgling sound coming from Sam's room. Alarmed – was he choking? – I went straight across and pushed the door open.

'Sam?' I whispered to the mound that was hidden under the duvet. From the shape of it, he seemed to be up on all fours, with his head buried under the pillow.

Up close, the sound was no less alarming. Was he retching? Was he vomiting? 'Sam?' I tried again, touching the mound now. 'You okay, love?'

He must have felt me because the duvet was immediately flung aside.

His cheeks were pink, his hair damp. But he was smiling at me. Beaming even. 'Is it morning?' he asked me. 'Is it getting-up time yet?'

'Well, yes, I suppose it is,' I said, 'but, Sam, sweetie, what were you doing? Are you okay? What were those noises I just heard?'

He looked confused for a moment, before comprehension dawned. 'I was just quiet howling,' he answered defensively. Then he looked suddenly crestfallen 'Oh, no – you heard me! You weren't supposed to! I still get my telly, don't I? Cos we never said I had to stop. Just that I had to be quiet. And I *was* quiet. Oh my God,' he said, slapping a hand against his forehead. 'Oh, why did you have to hear me? *Why*?'

Here we go, I thought, watching his expression change. *Here comes the next meltdown*. I could have kicked myself, too. Why did I rush in the way I had?

Though I knew I was thinking with the benefit of hindsight. I'd only rushed in because I was worried something was wrong. But cometh the hour, cometh the moment of inspiration. Perhaps I should try a different tack?

I threw my head back. 'Ah wooooo!' I went. 'Ah woooooooh!'

Sam stared at me as though I'd gone completely mad. And spurred on by his reaction – or, rather, lack of negative reaction – I tightened my dressing-gown belt and stepped up onto his bed.

He looked stunned.

'Come on,' I urged, planting my feet apart for stability. 'I'm up now, so let's do some proper howling, shall we?' I held out my hands. 'Come on, both of us. And let's have a bounce while we're at it. It's been ages since I had a proper bounce on a bed.'

'Really?' he asked, looking up at me doubtfully.

'Yes, really,' I said, grabbing his hands. 'Come on – ah woooooooh!'

And he did. And I reflected on my good choice in divan beds, as it took the strain of my not-so-tiny bouncing, howling body, and we bounced and howled, laughing, for several surreal minutes – at least till Tyler appeared in the doorway.

'What the *hell*, Mum?' he said. 'And I thought I'd seen everything.'

'Tyler, Tyler!' sang Sam. 'Come up! Come and howl with us!'

Tyler smiled at him. 'I'd break your bed, mate.' Then to me. 'Seriously, I really *have* seen it all now.'

'And that's all you're going to see for now,' I said, jumping down again. 'Not least because I'm completely puffed. Come on, love,' I said to Sam. 'Enough bouncing for today, I think.'

He let me help him down, as Tyler – with an eye-roll – headed off to the bathroom, then tugged at the sleeve of my dressing gown.

'So am I allowed to howl again properly now, Casey? I don't get it.'

I patted his head. 'Like you said, sweetie, we never said you *couldn't* howl – just that you had to be quiet till the grown-ups were awake. And I was awake, so that was fine.'

'So shall we do it again tomorrow?' he asked, and his face was as eager as a puppy's. 'I can knock on your door first, if you like. You can howl with me *every* morning if you want to.'

It was all too easy to picture it. And all too easy to see why Tyler told everyone he lived in a madhouse. But I had averted a meltdown, so it was a productive type of madhouse. Well, at least for the moment.

In the world of fostering, little moments like those really mattered. They were what I fondly called my 'little bits of happy', and that morning's little bit of happy seemed to set the tone for the rest of the morning. By the time Sam's allocated social worker, Colin Sampson, telephoned me (Christine Bolton had told me to expect to hear from him mid-morning) I was feeling more upbeat than I had at any time since Sam had arrived.

'I'm so sorry about being away,' he said, once he'd introduced himself. 'Not an ideal situation, is it?'

He sounded very young, and a little nervous, too – and I imagined the two were probably related. 'Oh, it's fine,' I reassured him. 'You couldn't know, could you? And everyone's entitled to their holidays,' I added, determinedly pushing all thoughts of sunshine and sea out of my mind. We would get our mini-break eventually. Besides, spring was definitely springing now, kicking winter into touch, finally, and the morning sun had further lightened my already lightened mood.

'Even so,' he persisted, 'I feel bad that you've been so unsupported up to now. Specially now I've had a chance to get properly up to speed. I've just come off the phone to Kelly and Steve. Hmmm. Complicated, by the sounds of it. So, how's it going with Sam now? Any progress?'

I looked across at the boy in question, who was sitting on the sofa quietly, looking through the big child's encyclopaedia that I had dug out for him. It was a pictorial one, filled with pictures and text aimed at much younger children, but he seemed to like it. He seemed engrossed in it, at least. Which was plenty for the moment. I took a couple of steps out into the hallway.

I lowered my voice. 'Better than you probably imagine, if you've already spoken to Steve and Kelly,' I told him. 'Which isn't to say that there aren't multiple challenges to be addressed.' I knew he'd have read my email updates (I had obviously been logging everything, daily and comprehensively) but gave him a quick summary of the main issues anyway; the meltdowns, the sudden rages, the instigation of the chart and so on – not least the early signs that it was having some effect.

'Chart?' he asked.

'Yes, we're using the old behaviour modification programme we were originally trained for.'

'What, like Pavlov's dogs?' So he had obviously studied psychology at some point.

'Kind of,' I admitted. 'Though perhaps a tiny bit more complex. It's essentially a system to help him with his behaviour issues using positive reinforcement.'

'I've not come across that yet,' he said.

'I'll run you through it when I see you. Though it takes time and perseverance, so don't expect instant miracles. Plus, we haven't really left the house with him yet,' I admitted. 'It could all go dramatically wrong when we try. But so far, so good. We've done a short walk to the park and survived that. So I'm on to the next step – my plan is to address that today. I'm going to take him out for pancakes at my sister's café. See how he copes with that before we venture further afield.'

'Good plan,' Colin said. 'All about little steps, isn't it? And it does sound as though it's going better than any of us would have expected, given his background. So, when can I pop round and meet him? Are you free at all next Monday?'

'I am,' I said, 'and I was wondering – have you heard anything yet about the possibility of a school for him? The days are marching on, and it can't be good him being out of education for all this time.'

'I believe ELAC are looking into it as we speak,' Colin confirmed. 'So keep your fingers crossed that we get something from them very soon. Perhaps even by the time I see you,' he added. Then he chuckled. 'Well, perhaps not – that's probably just my holiday brain talking, isn't it?'

I agreed that it was but, nevertheless, felt quite positive as I ended the call. ELAC – Education for Looked After Children – had avenues into schools for children in care that other 'mere mortals' didn't. And that was because if a child was in care, the normal obstacles to getting them into a school often didn't apply. Just because they'd been out of education for a while, or had been excluded in the past, didn't mean they couldn't quickly be put on roll at a local primary; schools, or special branches of schools in an alternative setting, weren't just helping out – they were legally obligated to provide looked-after children with some form of learning. As they needed to be – some of those children weren't the kind schools would be exactly fighting to admit, after all.

So, two little bits of happy to start my day with. Progress – a school for Sam might already be on the horizon, and with the chart seeming to be working, and the outbursts becoming less violent and less frequent, I was also puffed up with pride. So much so that I pushed away the tiny thought that popped into my head: my mother's voice whispering, 'You know what pride comes before, don't you, Casey?'

'Come on then, kiddo,' I said to Sam, as I returned to the living room and grabbed my bag from the back of the chair. 'Let's get our coats on and get on the road. I promised you pancakes at a café once I'd had my phone call, and that's what we shall have.'

He nodded towards the television, which was now on, the book having been discarded. 'But I'm watching *Fireman Sam* now,' he said plaintively. 'Can't we just stay in?'

'Well,' I said, immediately clocking signs that a meltdown might be imminent. 'We *could* do that, I suppose, but equally, we could pause it where it is, go to Truly Scrumptious, get pancakes with strawberries and chocolate, stuff our faces, and then rush back to finish off watching *Fireman Sam* afterwards?'

It was touch and go. His body was already stiffening as I watched him – a kind of physical 'hum' of trapped energy. Then he started to shake, head to foot, and his hands bunched into fists. But at the same time I could tell he was trying to contain it; breathing deeply, in and out, just as Mike had shown him several times, and eventually succeeding in keeping the lid on himself. At least for the moment. 'Okay,' he said finally. 'As long as we're quick. One, two, three, four, five, six, seven, eight …'

He continued to count – strands of his hair, it seemed – as I helped him into his coat. And continued to do so, as we went out, and he climbed into the car.

'You know,' I said as I strapped him in (sixty-seven, sixty-eight …), 'instead of counting all the way to a hundred when you're stressed or angry, you could try counting to ten or twenty instead. You might find it's better. It might help you calm down a bit faster.'

It was as if I'd just burned him. He jolted back into his seat, looking terrified. 'Where are we *really* going?' he demanded.

'To where I said,' I replied, surprised by the intensity of his sudden fear. 'Truly Scrumptious. Remember? My sister's café? For pancakes?'

'*Really*?'

'Yes, *really*,' I said, shutting the door and going round to get in myself. 'Why ever wouldn't we, when they do the best pancakes in town?' I adjusted my rear-view mirror so I could see him. 'So, you know, you don't need to count at *all*, silly sausage. And you know what else? You just did a *very* good thing. You were upset that you couldn't finish your programme – I could see that – but you calmed yourself down enough to do the right thing. That was *really* clever of you. You should be proud. Because I'm very, very proud of you. Anyway,' I added, smiling at him before re-adjusting the mirror, 'pancakes here we come, eh? I'm getting a stack of four. How about you?'

He shrugged, looking gloomy now. Like a condemned man going to the gallows. Something had changed, and there was another hurdle ahead of us. I just knew it. 'I'm not counting mine,' he said sullenly. 'You can count them if you want.'

And I must count my blessings, I told myself as we drove off. And *not* count on all being well when we got there. Little steps, just as Colin had pointed out.

But, as it turned out, Sam had another surprise up his sleeve. He was biddable enough as we entered the café, and polite enough when Donna greeted us, and showed us, with great ceremony, to her 'special table' right by the window. He even showed a modicum of interest in his pancakes, which I hoped might 'jolly' him out of his current sulky mood, and reveal to my sister the sunny, happy child he'd been earlier.

But I was wrong. What was about to happen – and it was something I could never have predicted – was that another facet of this many-sided child was showing up.

There was an elderly lady sitting alone at an adjacent table, and as is the way of elderly ladies everywhere, she leaned across, obviously charmed by Sam's sweet, winsome looks.

'Someone's enjoying their lunch,' she observed, with a smile. 'I'd put on half a stone if I even looked at something with that much cream on.'

Sam turned towards her, his spoon hovering midway to his mouth. 'Stop looking at me,' he said, smiling. 'You fucking freak.'

I was shocked as much by the smile as the words that had come from his mouth.

'Sam!' I said, cringing at the poor woman's horrified expression. 'What on *earth* did you say that for? Please say sorry to the lady.'

In answer, he shoved the spoonful of pancake into his mouth and spoke through it. 'She knows what will happen if she carries on,' he said. But said it *so* matter of factly – no threatening tone, no aggression. No sense, as far as I could see, that he'd even said anything wrong.

I was flabbergasted. 'I'm so *sorry*,' I said to the woman. 'I really don't know what else to say to you. Sam, *really*. Come on, now. Say sorry, please.'

'But I'm eating,' he answered levelly. And eat he did, too. Shovelling spoonfuls into his mouth as if his life now depended on it.

I mouthed another apology, but it was clear that the lady could already see my consternation. And aided by some sort of sign language from my sister (the lady was obviously a regular) that she understood that my charge wasn't an 'everyday' kind of little boy.

I didn't doubt that Donna would soon fill her in properly – she'd been round this particular block with me many times before, after all. And in the meantime Sam continued to eat his pancakes, seemingly oblivious. And as I returned to eating my own, I knew two things for certain – one, that I had barely scratched the surface with this child, and two, that I should always heed the truth of my mother's words.

Chapter 7

I didn't dwell on Sam's unexpected utterance at my sister's café. As with toddlers who've picked up an unsavoury expression, the rule of thumb was generally to ignore it; paying too much attention to an undesirable behaviour in an attempt to stop it happening could end up having the opposite effect, and reinforcing it.

Though Sam wasn't a toddler. And the fact still remained that it wasn't so much what he'd said but the way he'd come out with it. He'd been entirely without emotion as he'd said those words, which had been odd, to say the least. Because as far as I could tell, there wasn't an iota of malice behind it, and it wasn't as if he'd been trying to look 'hard', either. He'd simply trotted the words out conversationally, as if he'd learned them by rote. And as he was the oldest child in the family it seemed reasonable to suppose not from his siblings, but perhaps an adult in his life.

I duly noted it, to add to my growing dossier of 'behaviours', and reflected that Monday, and Colin's visit, really couldn't come soon enough, as the black hole where a picture of Sam's background should be was growing deeper by the day. I could only hope that in the intervening days Colin would have done a little digging.

In the meantime, it was business as usual. And as the general trajectory was up rather than downhill, I decided to take the plunge and expand Sam's social circle; while all the males in the family were off watching Kieron play football on Saturday, I suggested Riley pop over and meet Sam, along with my granddaughter, Marley Mae. It seemed the safest bet (I was still mindful of the challenges that might be posed by unfamiliar visitors), since Riley, both because of her innate personality and because she was a fellow foster carer now, was fazed by almost nothing. And Marley Mae, being her mother's daughter and a little girl with two older brothers, was used to being around boisterous older boys.

And, as I'd expected, she marched in with her usual breezy confidence.

'I'm Marley Mae,' she announced when we ushered her in to meet Sam. 'I'm five, nearly thix, and I already got my firth wobbly tooth. Look, ith *here*!' she added, opening her mouth to illustrate.

Sam duly peered in and nodded, as Marley Mae jiggled it with her finger. He then opened his own mouth and grimaced to show his teeth off as well. 'I've got big teeth,' he said. 'You're gonna grow some like these now.'

Riley and I exchanged smiles. So far, at least, so good. And Marley Mae was clearly impressed. 'Ooh, they're *big* teeth,' she agreed. Then, in a smooth, if bizarre, segue, added, 'and are you a good boy or a bad boy? Nanny sometimes has bad boys in, doesn't she, Mamma?'

Sam looked up at me, as if for direction on how to answer.

'Oh *course* Sam's a good boy,' Riley said before he or I could. 'What a question to ask, madam! Now, come on, let's get your coat off while Nanny sorts out something for you to play with.'

Sam didn't seem to mind either way – in fact, he looked enthused by the prospect of a playmate, dashing off to retrieve his encyclopaedia. 'She can look at my book with me if she wants,' he said, as he fetched it. 'There's lots of pictures and I know *lots* of the words. I can read to her like they do on the telly if you want.'

'Oh, I'm sure she *does* want,' said Riley. 'You'd like that, wouldn't you, princess? Marley's brothers aren't very good at reading to her,' she added to Sam, *sotto voce*, 'so you will *definitely* be in her good books if you do that. And in mine too, for that matter, because I get five minutes' peace.'

Sam looked puffed up with pride as he fussed over floor cushions, and within moments they were both sitting poring over the big, colourful pages, creating a tableau as sweet and normal as any you could imagine – Sam seemingly nothing like the child who'd arrived with us two weeks ago. As Riley was quick to point out.

'Well, he seems really sweet,' she said, as we watched them, while sipping coffee, having retired to the adjacent dining-room area where I could still keep a close eye. 'Nothing remotely like the picture you've been painting,' she added. 'I was expecting a little monster, not a little angel.'

'Appearances can be deceptive,' I pointed out. 'There are many sides to Sam, believe me – none of which tend to remain in residence for long. He's such a puzzle, he really is. Not least because I still know barely anything about him. Or what to expect from him. And that's literally on a minute-by-minute basis.'

Though as it turned out, contrary to the five minutes' peace Riley had been hoping for, Sam obliged us by giving us a whole twenty of them. And it was with impeccable timing that he then kicked off with my granddaughter, because it happened just as Riley was commenting that I'd obviously worked miracles. (That pride thing was working overtime, clearly.)

'Oh,' he suddenly said, rising to his feet and planting a hand on each hip. 'So you want to play a different game, do you?'

'Yeth, I *do* –' Marley Mae began, adding a pout for good measure. 'This one's boring. I want –'

'Well, I've got a *different* game,' he continued, 'How about I lock you in the dog cage and leave you in there till you've pissed your *pants*? How d'you think you'd like *that*?'

Riley and I rose up as one from the dining table. But Marley Mae, being Marley Mae, already had this verbal assault covered. She scrambled up as well, casting the book aside, and squared up to Sam. He had a couple of inches on her, but no more than that – certainly not enough to make her think twice. She was used to shouting brothers down after all. 'Oh, you are *such* a naughty boy, Sam!' she said, her hands also on her hips now. 'You just did a bad word, and you're *for* it!'

I stepped in between the two of them at the same time as Riley swooped in and picked Marley Mae up, who wriggled indignantly as she was ushered off to the kitchen.

'He did, Mummy!' I could hear her protesting, 'Cross my heart, he *did*!'

I leaned down towards the culprit, who seemed as stunned as anyone else. 'Sam,' I said, keeping my voice level, 'we do not use swear words in this house. You know that. And why were you being so mean to Marley Mae? What's all this about a dog cage? What a mean thing to say to a little girl.'

I'd grown to expect the unexpected, but as it had been over a week since he'd done it, it was unexpected nevertheless when he shot a hand out, grabbed a hank of my hair, and tugged on it, really hard. 'I hate you!' he said. I noticed his eyes were full of tears now. 'My game was a *good* game, and she wouldn't play it! And I hate her as well! She's just *lame*.'

I prised my hair from Sam's fingers and counted mentally to ten. 'Enough of all this "hate" stuff,' I told him firmly. 'That's my granddaughter you are talking about, young man, and I will not tolerate you using that kind of language about her. Now go up to your room, please – and you can stay there for thirty minutes to have a good think about what just happened here, okay? Go on. *Now!*'

The tone of my voice must have alerted some instinct because, rather than retaliate, Sam – whose tears had now plopped onto his cheeks – simply glared at me and stomped off into the hall. I heard him thundering up the stairs and then the slam of his bedroom door, beyond which I knew he'd be counting away furiously.

In the meantime my priority was to comfort my granddaughter, whose sobs – in all likelihood of frustration rather than distress, admittedly – were by now loud enough to wake the dead.

Though she was fine. She was wrapped, koala-style, around Riley's hip, and when she saw me she smiled immediately and put her arms out for a cuddle. She was a robust child and I knew she'd probably been piqued more than anything; she'd suffered far worse verbal onslaughts from her brothers. (Who I didn't doubt she'd be telling all to, in great detail, just as soon as they got home from football. Not to mention her own school friends, come Monday. Such was life.)

But though I was still mindful of what Mike had said about the grandchildren being impacted on, my thoughts were more about what Sam had actually said. As with what he'd said in Donna's café, it was as if he was reciting something *he'd* heard – clearly a threat that had been made to him. And made often? Clearly often enough that he'd assimilated it into his own repertoire of rebukes. So had he been locked in that cage often too? It seemed reasonable to assume yes. I couldn't wait to find out more about where he came from.

Riley, though, was more interested in the here and now of Sam's chart, which was glistening with its rows of silver stars. She nodded towards it. 'So I'm guessing you'll be docking him some of these today,' she commented.

'Yesh, Nanna – because he's *bad*,' added Marley Mae, sagely.

I set her down on the worktop and went across to the store cupboard to fetch her a biscuit. 'He's not a bad *boy*, sweetie,' I told her. 'He's a boy who did a bad *thing*. Which is different. Now, then, which one d'you fancy? A jammy one? A wafer?'

She chose a wafer and went across to the table to do some colouring. Riley, however, was still looking at the chart. 'So he's properly on the programme, is he? I thought you told me they weren't funding this thing anymore.'

'They're not. But I'm doing it anyway. Christine suggested it, actually.'

'I thought you said she didn't think much of it?'

'Apparently not so. She just didn't really know anything about it. But she's canny – I think she knew suggesting I try it might make me more likely to take him.'

Riley chuckled. 'And she was right, wasn't she?'

'One hundred per cent. I'm mean, he's the ideal child for it, isn't he? Well, so far.' I grinned ruefully. 'Still early days, obviously. And no, he won't lose any stars. Going to his room is his punishment. You remember how it works, don't you?'

'Kind of,' Riley said. 'Though I'm not sure I really get it. How come he still gets all this stuff? I mean, isn't that like rewarding a kid for bad behaviour?'

To be fair, I doubted Riley would remember how it worked in the early stages. She'd come into fostering later, at a time when such 'new-fangled' regimes had gone out of fashion (as all new initiatives tend to when money is tight). And though she was now doing respite work pretty regularly, up to now she and David hadn't taken on the sort of children for whom this sort of behaviour-management programme was indicated. And wouldn't, either, not while her own were still so young. And, given Kelly and Steve's experience with Sam, I was grateful for that.

'I know it seems counterintuitive,' I said, 'but, at least at this stage, with this sort of child, it's not a reward/punishment scenario. It's completely unconnected with what he does wrong. It's all about the positives – what he *achieves*. What he succeeds at.'

'Well, as long as he doesn't succeed in sending you loopy in the process, Mum, like Miller did. Anyway,' she lowered her voice a little, 'what was all that stuff about a dog cage? Do you know the background?'

I lowered my own voice. 'Only that he was found in the one in the family's garden. And that it looks like he spent a lot of time locked in there – his siblings were convinced that he thought he was a dog. I told you about the howling thing he does, didn't I?'

Riley nodded. 'And you still think he has autism?'

'Absolutely, yes. Though I think there's something else going on, too. I just can't put my finger on what, quite.'

Riley grinned. 'Busy sleuthing already, Mother?'

I smiled back at her. 'Is the Pope Catholic? But seriously, I do.'

'Perhaps – let me see now – being locked in a dog cage in a garden on a regular basis?'

'Well, that's obviously one worrying aspect,' I agreed.

But was it actually 'worrying', or was I playing dog myself, and busily barking up the wrong tree?

Because, once again, Sam threw a spanner in my detective work. Once Riley and Marley Mae had left I went straight up to check on him, to find him laid out like a sardine, not in, but *underneath* his bed. I don't know how many times he'd counted to one hundred since I'd sent him up there, but he was midway in counting to it now.

I got down on my knees and peered into the murk. 'What on earth are you doing under there?' I asked him.

He carried on counting, moving his fingers across the flecks in the carpet.

'Sam?'

'Shh!'

So I shushed, till he reached the magic hundred. 'Come on,' I said, once he was done, 'wriggle out, so we can have a proper chat.'

He shook his head. Then turned towards me. 'Casey,'

he said, his eyes gleaming bright in the darkness, 'you know the treats list?'

'On your chart?'

'Can we have an extra one on there? For, like, if I'm really, really good?'

I considered for a moment. 'I don't see why not,' I said.

'I know I can't have a dog, but I'd really, really love a dog cage.'

'A *dog cage*?'

A nod.

'Like the one you had at home?'

Another nod. A tearful sniff. 'It's just I really, really miss it.'

I sat back on my haunches, and made a mental note to get all this down, ready for Colin's visit on Monday. He *missed* it?

As Alice said, this was getting curiouser and curiouser.

Chapter 8

And it carried on getting curiouser and curiouser, because Sunday proved odd in yet another way. It started normally enough. Even better than normally, in fact, first because I got a lie-in, and second because I was woken up by Tyler, bearing a bacon sandwich and a mug of coffee.

'Here you go,' he said, handing me the morning paper as well. 'Compliments of Dad for the Queen of Sheba. Go on, knock yourself out.'

'Okay, spill,' I said, sitting up. 'Because it's definitely not my birthday. So which is it? Have the pair of you broken something or burnt down half the house?'

His expression became pained. 'Harsh, Mother. *Harsh*. Dad just thought he'd leave you to it while he goes through his paperwork. He's got that course thingy to do this morning, hasn't he?'

Of course. Now I remembered – another responsibility of senior management. Mike had to deliver a Health and Safety presentation to some new employees at the factory

– something to do with forklift manoeuvring, as I remembered, and what to do with hazardous waste. Which, despite him knowing a lot about both, really wasn't his sort of thing at all. Not least because it involved two of his least favourite things – speaking to an audience and getting togged up in a suit.

'Ah, of course,' I said. 'Bless him. And what's Sam up to?'

'He's fine. He's with me.' Tyler nodded back towards his own room. 'We're playing on the PlayStation. On which note, I'd better get back before he finishes his level. Enjoy, Ma'am,' he added, with a sweep of the arm and a bow.

'Oh, don't worry,' I said, stretching luxuriously. 'I intend to. Oh,' I added as he turned to go, 'and you can bring me my second cup in, say, fifteen minutes?'

Fortunately there was no cushion to hand for him to throw at me.

Though it was Mike himself who came in, not fifteen but twenty minutes later, bearing the expression of a man for whom the word 'hazardous' had taken on an entirely different meaning. He looked like a man with too much on his mind.

'God, I *hate* this sort of thing,' he muttered as he started assembling his new temporary persona, rummaging in the bottom of the wardrobe for his only pair of 'good' shoes, and in the chest of drawers for a pair of black socks. 'Why can't they just email everyone the flipping guidelines? Why do I have to stand there doing a bloody PowerPoint presentation?'

'Love, you'll be *fine*,' I said. 'You're not exactly giving a speech to the United Nations. It's just going through some protocols with a handful of blokes.'

'Oh, I know,' he said. 'It's just the whole "being on show" thing I hate. It's just so not me.'

'I know, love. But I'm sure you'll be fine once –'

'What the *hell*?' he interrupted.

'What the hell what?' I asked, as he held a shirt aloft on its hanger – one he'd just plucked from the rail in the wardrobe.

'This,' he said, bringing it over to me. 'Where the hell are all the buttons?'

'Buttons?' I inspected it. And he was right: there were none.

'Well, there were definitely buttons on it when I ironed it,' I said. But he'd already thrown it on the bed and returned to the wardrobe. Where out came a second shirt, then a third, then another, then, lastly, in desperation, even his dress shirt. (Mike was not a man with much need for formal shirts.) 'Every one of them,' he said, and I could sense his rising panic. 'Not a single button between them – not even on the cuffs!'

I'd scrambled out from under the duvet to take a proper look myself now. 'Well, that's just mad …' I said, checking them for myself. Then I glanced across the landing, immediately thinking 'Sam'. Because what else was there *to* think? Because unless some new genetically modified strain of them had fluttered across the English Channel,

I was fairly sure clothes moths didn't much care for shirt buttons. 'I wonder if –'

'Case, this is a *crisis*. What the hell am I going to *wear*? Because I'm obviously not going to fit into any of Tyler's, am I?' He started rummaging in the wardrobe again, pushing hangers back and forth. 'Or your blouses for that matter. Case, what am I going to *do*?'

I was on my feet now and, happily, thinking on them too. 'I know!' I said, having had a eureka moment. 'There's that charity bag in the airing cupboard after my loft sort-out last month. I'm almost certain there are a couple of Kieron's old shirts in there. Hang on, let me go and check. Ty!' I added, raising my voice as I headed for the landing. 'Can you do me a massive, massive favour?'

His head appeared from his bedroom door. 'Woo, Mother,' he said, looking at my frazzled expression. 'Where's the fire?'

'No fire, just having to do a bit of emergency firefighting. Can you run down and pop the ironing board up and put the iron on for me, sweetie? We have an emergency shirt-ironing situation. Well, at least if I can find one,' I added as I flung open the airing-cupboard door, and got my hand on the half-filled charity bag in question.

Sam himself, who I could see was still engrossed in the game in Tyler's bedroom, seemed oblivious to the panic playing out on the landing. Truly engrossed, or just faking it? Either way, for Mike, the got-to-be-on-time-at-work clock was ticking. I'd have to deal with him later.

* * *

'Case, I can't wear *that*!' Mike exclaimed minutes later, when he appeared in the conservatory, togged up in only trousers, socks and shoes, and with his tie and suit jacket over his arm. 'And that was *Kieron's*?' he asked, pointing to the shirt I'd just finished ironing. 'He actually went out in public wearing *that*?' He shook his head. 'Because if he did, I'm pretty sure I'd have remembered. Because I would have told him he looked like a bloody *girl*! Look at it! It's got flowers all over it!'

He was right, of course. It had. But at least they were small, discreet, monochrome flowers. Though I naturally didn't add that, as far as I knew, Kieron had never worn it either – it being a present from his partner Laura, back in the days when she thought she could 'snazz up' his wardrobe. Which hadn't worked, despite her best efforts. Though, for the record, I was with Laura on the style front; I rather liked it. What on earth was wrong with men wearing flowers, anyway? It wasn't like he'd be wearing them behind his ear.

'Dad, it's *fine*,' Tyler said, clearly seeing the need for some encouragement. '*Loads* of lads wear flowery shirts these days. No, *really*, Dad. *Honest*. I reckon it'll make you look cool more than anything.'

'Son, cool is not something I aspire to looking *any* day, let alone one when I'm supposed to look like the flipping boss.'

'Er, hello?' Tyler said. 'What about Richard Branson?'

Mike glared at him. 'What's Richard Branson got to do with it?'

'He wears horrible hairy jumpers and he's a zillionaire, isn't he?'

'Oh, for God's sake,' I interjected, 'just put the bloody thing on, will you? Far better to be in a flowery shirt than be late.'

'Which I'll *never* live down,' he grumbled, as he shrugged himself into it.

'Dad, you'll look *sick*,' Tyler added, working hard to stop his mouth twitching.

'Plus it's Sunday,' I pointed out. 'It's fine to dress down a little on a Sunday.' I handed him his jacket before he could protest further. 'Here, put this on. I think you'll be pleasantly surprised when you see yourself, actually.'

'Case, trust me, the last thing – the very *last* thing – I intend to do is look in a mirror. If I get so much as a *glimpse* I won't even be able to leave the house.'

'Dad, seriously,' Tyler said. 'You look *fine*. You look sick.'

Mike scowled as he picked up his car key and papers. 'Not as sick,' he said wretchedly, 'as I *feel*.'

'So what's all that about?' Tyler asked, once we'd waved off our reluctant 'new man'. (Who, for what it was worth, I too thought looked rather 'sick'.) 'Where have all Dad's shirt buttons gone anyway? You think it was Sam?' He glanced towards upstairs. 'You think he took them?'

'I'm not sure what to think, love,' I said. 'But I can't see who else could have cut them off, can you? Still, there's only one way to find out …' We both headed up the stairs.

A Dark Secret

I was used to things going missing, of course. A sizeable proportion of the children we'd taken care of down the years had stolen things from us. Some big and serious, others small and insignificant. One child several years back had even extended his operations to encompass climbing out of his bedroom window, and into other bedroom windows, so he could pilfer things from our neighbours, as well. It was, as they say, all par for the course. Some of those kids came from backgrounds where stealing was commonplace, others from situations – and emotional conditions – that meant they stole without even really realising what they were doing, or to satisfy some deep psychological need. Our first foster child, Justin, had been so neglected when he'd come to us that he had a habit of stockpiling small items of food. He really was that anxious about where his next meal might come from that when food was placed in front of him he would gorge himself like a starving animal, and if he saw food he could stuff in his pockets for later, he couldn't stop himself from doing so and hiding it away. I'd discovered it all hidden away under his bed, in his suitcase, months later. So much stuff that it was as if he was preparing for an apocalypse.

But why on earth would Sam steal all Mike's shirt buttons? And when had he done it? *How* could he have done it? Did we have yet another night-time ninja under our roof?

We got upstairs to find Sam was no longer in Tyler's bedroom. He'd not followed us down during the short kerfuffle, but clearly hadn't stayed playing the game either – evidence, even if circumstantial, of his guilt?

'I'll get this, love,' I told Tyler, who was soon to go out and meet his friends. 'You go off and get yourself ready.'

He nodded. 'Will do,' he whispered. 'Good luck with button-gate!'

I had to admit there was a comedic element to it all – not least the idea that our little guest had been creeping around in search of shirt buttons, like an industrious elf out of a fairy tale by the Brothers Grimm. But there was a serious element too; it was such an odd thing to do, and as if I needed further proof of the complexity of Sam's psyche, here it undoubtedly was. I found him back in his own bedroom, and I could tell by his expression that he knew the game was up, too. But what *was* the game?

He'd been sitting cross-legged on his bed but he immediately jumped off. 'D'you need me to wash the dishes or something?' he asked. He was trying for innocence in his tone, but it wasn't really working – the pink spots on his cheeks gave him away.

'No, Sam, but I do need to know why you've cut the buttons off all Mike's shirts. Why would you do that?'

'I never,' he said immediately.

'Sam, remember what I've told you about always telling the truth?'

'I never,' he said again, a little more shrilly. A stance slightly undermined by the way his gaze kept darting to the left of me, to where the chest of drawers stood.

'Really, Sam?'

'I never!' he said a third time, his gaze still going back and forth – as if he was a felon calculating angles so he could plan a swift escape. Or, more likely, to stop me from looking in a particular place.

'Well, if that's so,' I said, 'then you won't mind me taking a quick look in your chest of drawers then, will you?'

This galvanised him. 'There's nothing in there! Just clothes and stuff! That's *all*.'

On the present showing he definitely wouldn't be making it as a criminal any time soon. And, as I stepped forward to do what I'd told him I was going to, he incriminated himself further by leaping in front of the chest and flinging his arms out to either side of him.

'There's nothing in here!' he went on, his voice rising in pitch now. 'Go away! Get off my stuff or I'll duff you, you hear me! Go away! There's just clothes, and they're *mine*!'

'Sam, I think we both know that isn't true,' I said, mentally crossing my fingers that I wouldn't be subjected to another physical assault. 'Come on, let me see …'

He kicked a foot out, which clipped my shin. 'Go away, or you're for it!'

I took a step back again, anxious to diffuse the situation. 'Okay,' I said. 'Then how about *you* show me what's in there? If it's just your clothes, fine. But, Sam, I think we both know why you're guarding it the way you are. Look, love,' I added softly, 'I just want to understand why you've done what you did.'

I thought he might lash out at me again and make a grab for my hair. His pinched expression suggested he was thinking about it, certainly. But he obviously (and this was progress in itself) debated his options and thought better of it. Instead, to my surprise, he threw himself down on the rug and swiftly rolled himself under his bed again. And, once he was tucked away, I heard the usual incantation; him beginning the count to one hundred.

Having dodged that particular bullet, I decided to leave him to it, and began pulling the drawers open one by one. And struck gold, finally, in the bottom-most. And there *was* gold – at least, pretend gold – and much else besides, because at the back of the drawer were half a dozen little 'nests'. Made from rolled-up socks and pants, each one contained its own kind of treasure; one held shirt buttons (so many shirt buttons – were some missing also from my blouses?), another sequins – that gold – which I recognised from an evening dress, a third held diamantes (so he'd been raiding my jewellery box as well?) and the remaining three held Lego bricks, sorted by colour – one of blue, one of red, one of white.

And, as Sam continued to quietly chant numbers from beneath the bed, I knew that if I chose one at random and counted the contents they would almost certainly amount to one hundred.

I sat back on my heels, considered my options for a moment, then lay down on the floor so I could be eye-to-eye with him.

'Sam,' I said, 'listen. Did you take all those things in your chest to count with?'

He carried on counting, only pausing to yell 'Go away!' at me before starting up where he left off. He jerked his nearest leg towards me for good measure.

I ignored both. 'Why are you counting, Sam?' I said calmly. 'Can you try and explain to me?'

There was an angry 'huff' of irritation between numbers. Then another. Then, unexpectedly, and loudly, 'Because I'm *scared*! Scared in my *head*!'

He spat the words out, then carried on counting.

'There is no reason to be scared, love,' I said. 'You're not going to be in trouble. You know you did wrong taking those things, but I'm more interested in *why* you took them.' And *when* and, for that matter, *how*, I thought.

It was a thought that led to another thought, which made me stand up again. I made another search and found a pair of nail scissors buried in his bedside cabinet, which he'd obviously purloined from the bathroom. Then, since he was still busy counting and showing no signs of stopping, I further inspected the diamantes he'd managed to gather, dismayed to see a couple that I recognised from a necklace I was very fond of, and a few I also knew came from a pair of cherished boots.

'I see he's speaking in tongues again,' Tyler whispered, popping his head around the bedroom door. He'd just had a shower and smelled of coconut shower gel. His gaze followed my pointing finger. 'Ah,' he said, 'so *that's* it. So he's like that other kid, isn't he? The one you told me about. The one with the tin of pebbles. Maybe you should go down and fetch him some,' he called back, as he headed into his own bedroom to dress.

Maybe I should, I thought, as I gathered up the diamantes and shirt buttons. The rest he could keep, including the sequins; I'd grown bored with the evening dress anyway, so it would be an excuse to buy a new one – well, if an occasion for one came up anytime soon. Which I had to concede was unlikely.

But Ty was clearly right. It was just like when we'd fostered Jensen and Georgie – the latter's collection of stones was his most cherished possession. And something that clearly had great emotional significance for him. He used them as a kind of charm, almost a form of protection, laying them across his bedroom doorway to deter people from going in his room, sometimes even creating a circle with them and sitting cross-legged in the centre, or putting some other treasured object in the middle, to keep it safe.

This was not that, quite. But it was further evidence of a self-soothing ritual. A device to make Sam's safe space feel even safer.

I got down on the bedroom floor again, and finally got his attention. 'Sam, you can't keep the gems,' I said. 'Or the shirt buttons, I'm afraid, because Mike obviously needs them. But I'm happy for you to keep the rest, okay? And perhaps, together, we can find some more things for you to count? Some pebbles from the garden, perhaps? Maybe some buttons from my button box? I have loads of buttons, so you could even make two sets, in different colours, if you like. What d'you say? How about we go on a "things-to-count" hunt? Like going on a treasure hunt, but without any pirates.'

He carried on counting, and those huge eyes peered out at me from the darkness. I could see the tears in them; a filmy sheen that glinted along his lash line.

'One hundred,' he said, finally. Then, just as I thought he'd start up again with 'one', out he rolled.

'But it'll be funner if we're pirates,' he observed, grinning as he tugged down his pyjama top.

As if absolutely nothing had happened.

Chapter 9

One of the many things I struggled to figure out about Sam was his ability to bounce back from his meltdowns. I mean, really bounce back, no matter what had happened. He could have a full-on violent episode, screaming like a banshee, and an hour later could be the sweetest kid ever. It happened every single time, which was obviously a plus, but could make it extremely difficult to explain to someone who hadn't witnessed it just how bad things could get. 'Think Jekyll and Hyde' didn't really cover it.

I knew, because I'd been on the other end of this. I'd thought the exact same thing myself when I'd first met Sam, hadn't I? I'd looked at the sweet kid who'd turned up on my doorstep, and had immediately thought (and against my better instincts, I'll admit) that Kelly might have been just a tad melodramatic. When he wasn't kicking off, Sam really was that endearing.

I was thinking exactly this on Monday morning when, with Colin Sampson's visit imminent, Sam was busy being

the proverbial little angel. And being angelic genuinely –
this wasn't some savvy youngster who'd spent a long time
in the system. Sam's sweetness and lightness was from
the heart.

'Sampson will be really pleased with me,' he declared,
as we added another silver star to the impressive rows of
them on the 'jobs' list on his chart. 'He'll say I'm a good
boy, won't he, Casey?'

'It's Colin, love,' I corrected. 'Sampson is his last name.
But yes, I'm quite sure he'll think you're a good boy,
because that's exactly what you are.'

Sam grinned like the Cheshire cat. 'Oh, yes,' he said. 'I
remember. But I like Sampson better than Colin because
it's got my name in it, hasn't it? And I bet he'll let me call
him that anyway, because Sampson was a big and strong
man from history. I told it to my little sister, because I
know the story.'

Do you now, I thought, marvelling at his random bits of
knowledge. He was almost certainly referring to the
biblical story, but for a child who seemed likely to
have attended school only intermittently, I wondered
where he had heard about it. Sunday school? Somehow I
doubted it.

And he'd mentioned his little sister. Something else to
note. All I knew of his siblings so far was that they were
called Will and Courtney, that they were seven and five
respectively, and that, even at this early stage, with all the
trauma they'd suffered, they were showing no signs of his
distinctive, and challenging, mental make-up. And that

Sam telling the latter stories was a world away from the relationship they had had latterly, sadly. He'd not mentioned either of them up to now, so this was quite a development, and I wanted to respond to it in such a way that he might tell me more. Give me some opening into the world of his childhood so far, which felt so unreachable and shut-away.

But there was no time to do so as the doorbell then rang. I would have to park it and leave it for later. Moments later I was opening the door to 'Sampson' himself – not so much big and strong as tall and reedy. Which didn't preclude him being strong, of course, but he didn't look the type to be taking on random lions. But that was fine too, because it was the establishment I was hoping he'd be taking on for me; a different kind of beast altogether. He also looked to be in his late twenties – thirty tops, I reckoned – and, with establishments, the energy of youth was usually a big plus.

'Come on in,' I said. 'Sam has been looking forward to meeting you. Look, he's even brushed his hair for you.'

Colin Sampson laughed as he followed us through to the dining area. 'Well at least that's one of us with neat hair today,' he said, smiling down at Sam as he ran his hands through his own windswept locks. 'I imagine I must look like I've been dragged through a hedge backwards. March winds, eh?' he added as he took off his quilted jacket.

Sam was right beside him, pulling a chair out, and sticking out his hand to shake. 'Can I call you Sampson, please, Mr Sampson?' he asked, as Colin took it and shook it firmly. 'Because I'm called Sam too, so it's like we're the same.'

'You know, Sam,' Colin said, 'I think I might like that. In fact, when I was at school, all my best friends used to call me Sampson.'

Sam's look could have melted glaciers, let alone ice cubes. 'I knew it!' he said happily. 'Casey, will you tell Sampson all about my really good stars?'

'I will do exactly that,' I said. 'In fact, in a bit, we'll all go into the kitchen and we'll even show him. But right now, I'm going to pop off and make some coffee and get the best biscuits out, while you two get to know each other a little bit better. Okay?'

With both happy to do so, I left the pair of them to it, feeling only the smallest pang of jealousy at Colin's holiday tan. Much as I missed the shot of sunshine I'd been looking forward to so much, it was at least spring now, and I was sure to get my mini-break eventually, and even more cheering was my first impression of Colin, which was overwhelmingly positive. He seemed cheerful and positive and, as I listened to them chatting and laughing in the other room, clearly a natural at getting along with troubled kids. Though I also found myself wondering if he'd read all my frantic emails already and was now forming the conclusion that I'd been making mountains out of molehills, as I'd done myself, once or twice, with Kelly.

'So,' Colin said as I set a laden tray down, 'our Sam here has been telling me all about his chart and how he's having a movie night this weekend with all the points he's totted up.'

I passed a mug of coffee across the table and took a seat myself. 'He is indeed,' I confirmed, 'and, you know what? I've just had a thought. I was thinking that if you wanted to win a pizza delivery with that movie, Sam, then maybe you could sit quietly for just fifteen minutes in your room now, while me and Colin get the boring paperwork out of the way.'

A shadow passed across Sam's face. He looked decidedly unconvinced by this new development. Even a little anxious. Something that was confirmed by his response of 'I don't have to do any counting, do I?' Which made me curse myself for not forewarning him about how the meeting was going to be conducted.

So I laughed. 'Heavens no, Sam! Just fifteen minutes of quiet reading while we go through all the dreary stuff. Why don't you take up the encyclopaedia and a couple of biscuits?' I pushed the plate towards him. 'Go on – any two you like.'

'Really?' he said, grabbing the two with shiny wrappers on (kids being the same everywhere) before toddling off up the stairs, great big book tucked under his stringy little arm.

'Full of beans, isn't he?' Colin said, after he was safely out of earshot. 'And the counting thing – I'd read about it in your emails. Interesting business. How's it going? Are things still proving challenging?'

I could tell by his tone that he wasn't challenging me, though. 'Not in the usual way,' I explained. 'As you've seen, he can be a poppet. I think the counting is mostly related to his autistic traits – it always seems to soothe him and help him – but the meltdowns are explosive, and I'm still trying to work his triggers out. Though right now I'm still unclear whether there are simply a lot of them or that it's just the one and I haven't got to grips with what it is yet. Though I'm no psychologist,' I added, 'which is why I'm so keen for him to see one.'

'You, the world and his wife,' Colin said, nodding ruefully. 'And, look, I'm so sorry I was away when Sam was allocated. But I'm on the case now – ahem – literally. So, what can I do to help? Is there any extra support I can give you? I'm obviously more than happy to start taking him off your hands for a couple of hours when I visit. All very well me reading emails and taking notes' – he had a notebook in front of him and had already been scribbling – 'but from what you've already told me I'm guessing some practical help wouldn't go amiss either.'

If I'd liked Colin on instinct, I liked him even more now. He was obviously what I thought of as one of the 'good' social workers. They were all good, of course, but, from my standpoint as a foster carer, some were more hands-on than others. I suppose it was the same as, on the flip side, social workers probably assessed us as well. Not a hard and fast rule, obviously, and I was always anxious not to stereotype, but, in my own experience, some were more 'theoretical' than others; using their training – all that theory – to inform the way they did the job, much more than the hands-on experiences of the foster carers they worked with.

Which was also fine. It was their job to manage their various cases the way they felt most appropriate, but, every once in a while, a 'Colin' came along – someone you just knew not only strove to understand and help the children they worked with, using their training and education, but also went the extra mile to empathise with us, the ones working at the coal-face, and to try and make our lives that little bit easier also.

I might have been way off-beam in my assessment, of course, but by the time we'd gone through the main events of the last couple of weeks, and the strategies I'd put in place for addressing them, I definitely had a good feeling about Colin Sampson.

'And, listen,' I said, 'now the team is complete, I'm feeling really positive. We're managing okay, I think – though some regular outings would be fallen upon with gratitude, as you can imagine – but now you're here, perhaps we can begin taking steps to get him into some form of education. Which I know means getting him formally assessed, and I know that won't be easy. But is there any slim hope of that happening anytime soon, do you think?'

'That's the biggest hurdle,' he agreed. 'And the request has been made. And I'm told it's being rushed through – well, as rushed as these things ever rush – but even when we get the results, and if the assumption is that Sam *is* on the spectrum, there's still going to be the difficulty of finding a specialist school near enough to you that will have a place for him, sad to say.'

I nodded. I already knew that. It was a constant and growing problem. Even Miller, our last child – with his multiple, urgent problems – had been out of education for months until a place had come up.

'I know,' Colin went on. 'But let's keep our fingers crossed. I can promise you I'll keep pushing for that assessment to happen soon, at least. And in the meantime, I'll try and support you as much as I can.' He nodded to the biscuits, before taking one and winking at me. 'Not least because bribery, as we all know, gets you everywhere.'

'That's good to know,' I said, grinning. 'And, for the record, I can also run to cakes. Though right now, I'm guessing you'll want to go and see Sam's bedroom. And also speak to him properly – and alone, of course – so why don't you head upstairs and kill two birds with one stone, while I go and dig out my lemon drizzle cake recipe?'

Colin took his notebook and pen and headed upstairs. As per the protocol, a social worker always needed to spend time alone with a child, new or not. A foster carer was never privy to these conversations, because, apart from anything else, it was an opportunity for a child to speak openly and honestly about how they were getting along in their placement, and what they really thought about their carers. If there were any issues or allegations as a result of these meetings then the carers would be told about them and given the chance to explain themselves.

But if anything serious cropped up, then, in some cases, the placement would be ended. This had never happened to us, thankfully, but making sure the child had the opportunity to feedback their experience of being fostered was a necessary part of a social worker's job, and rightly so.

In this case it appeared that all was good, bordering on very good, because when they emerged half an hour later, Sam was, if possible, full of even more beans.

'Casey! Casey!' he shouted as he bounded down the stairs, 'Sampson thinks I'd make a *very* good dog person, don't you, Sampson?'

'Yes, I do,' he said, following at a more sedate pace, 'but I also said that when you grow up would be a good time to get your very own dog, didn't I? Sam here was telling me all about his dog, Brucie,' he explained to me. 'And how sad he'd been that he'd died when he was still only a puppy.'

This was news. Useful news. Contradictory news, too. 'Oh, love, I didn't know that,' I said. 'I thought you never had a dog. That *is* sad. I'm so sorry.'

Sam nodded, looking sad, seemingly having forgotten he'd told me otherwise. 'Brucie was my dog. His real name was Bruce but he got out of the garden and was runned over because his cage wasn't locked.'

Ah, I thought. *Ah*. Perhaps that had been why – because he felt partly responsible. 'I tell you what, Sam,' I said, 'I've been thinking while you've been upstairs. And I happen to know that our Kieron isn't working today, so if

98

you like we can call down to his house after lunch and ask if we can take Luna out for a walk in the park or something. Would you like that? Luna is my son's Westie,' I added for Colin's benefit. 'The word "walkies" is her favourite in the entire dictionary.'

'Well, that sounds like an excellent idea,' Colin said as he slipped his jacket off the newel post. 'And while you're off doing that, I'll go back to the office and check if they've left any spaces in my diary. I'll come and visit you in the next week or so, Sam, okay? So have a think about the sort of thing you'd like us to do.'

'I like doing *everything*,' Sam told him, beaming.

And Sam certainly seemed to love Luna. As it turned out, we got out later than we'd planned, so by the time we'd driven over to Kieron's he'd had to pop out to collect Dee Dee from school and take her to her dance class straight after. So he'd texted me to tell me to let myself in, take Luna and drive back to mine to walk her. He'd come and pick her up from us on his way home again. So half an hour after that, Sam and I (him as excited as a puppy himself) set off to the park and woods at the end of our road, on what had turned out, though still windy, to be a lovely bright spring afternoon.

I'd been here many, many times before, of course. It was one of the main reasons we'd come to love living where we did so much. We'd moved to our current home several years back, in circumstances that weren't exactly ideal (it had been with a heavy heart, and we'd only done so because of a previous foster child we'd cared for), but we'd settled in really quickly, not least because of the lovely (and, happily, tolerant) neighbours, plus the beautiful green space that was just a walk away. I'd brought previous foster children here, and my own grandchildren, obviously, who loved the woods and the play area and – best of all – being able to paddle in the small stream which ran through it.

And, as soon as we set off, I could tell straight away that to bring Sam here, perhaps daily – at least till a school was found for him – would potentially be a good thing for him too; not least to wear him out a bit and perhaps, as a result, take the edge off his rages and meltdowns.

We'd brought Luna's ball, and her plastic ball-throwing doohickey. I carried the latter, while Sam took charge of lead duties, thrilled to be responsible for extending the line, and reeling her back in again to cross the road.

'This is *wicked*,' he enthused, as if it was the best invention ever. 'It's like she can be on the lead but *off* the lead all at once. I think all dogs should be given them, on the Health Service.'

It was such a funny little thing to say that I almost laughed out loud. And did, when he declared the ball-throwing device to be, in contrast, the *worst* invention ever. 'Why can't people throw with their actual *arms*?' he wanted to know. 'Doing it with that thing's so *lazy*.'

I could only agree, so we abandoned the ball-throwing doohickey, and as I watched him enjoy the simple pleasure of spending time with Kieron's dog, I was reminded of the oft-quoted truism about animals – that they really could be good for the soul. And for this little troubled soul, definitely.

And as is so often the case when you're out with a dog, we passed other dogs, and other owners I knew. And one dog in particular, a Collie called Flame, who lived on our street, but who was tugging on his lead in his enthusiasm to say hello, but from the grip of an unexpected owner.

Flame was owned by a lady who lived a few doors down called Mrs Pegg, but he was in the charge of a teenager I didn't recognise. At least, I thought I didn't, but when he caught up with his overexcited canine, I realised his face was familiar from somewhere.

And I was right. He was Mrs Pegg's grandson, Oliver. 'She's recovering from surgery,' he explained, when I asked how she was. 'She got her knee-replacement operation moved forward.'

I knew my neighbour was on the waiting list but, as with knee operations everywhere, had assumed it would be months away yet.

'Is she okay?' I asked. 'Does she need anything?'

'She's fine,' Oliver said. 'Just can't walk much for a bit, obviously.' He made a grab for Flame's lead so he wouldn't trample Luna in his excitement. Then smiled wryly. 'In the meantime, we've got a rota.'

'What's a rota?' Sam piped up.

'Like a chart,' I explained. 'With a list of who's supposed to do what and when.'

'I've got a chart! I've got a chart!' Sam trilled to Oliver. 'I do lots of different things when I'm supposed to as well. And when I do them I get a star on it. Do you?'

Oliver shook his head. 'No, just one of my nan's "brownie points",' he said, chuckling.

'And her undying gratitude,' I added. 'Of that I'm sure. Will you tell her I'll pop over to see her later?'

And as we parted, and I made a mental note to do just that, I reflected that while Sam had his chart, I had something equally useful.

An idea.

Chapter 10

My dog-walking idea proved to be a winner. Not only did I have the undying gratitude of my neighbour's grandson, but, as far as I could fathom Sam's complicated personality, I felt I'd really turned a corner with him, at least in knowing what made him happy, because walking Flame seemed to make him very happy indeed.

It also provided an outlet for his need to howl and bark and, though we attracted the odd sideways look when Sam launched into an episode, most didn't even bat an eyelid – he was just a nine-year-old boy, out with a dog, who was pretending to be a dog. As for the dog himself, well, he seemed to enjoy it too.

Our new regime of daily dog walks also proved to be a much-needed distraction from all the waiting around for news from the various authorities. Although meeting Colin Sampson had been uplifting, and a very positive experience, I still knew that all the reams of red tape dictated that we had a long road ahead. There were lots of unanswered questions and only certain professionals had the authority to answer them. CAMHS – Child and Adolsescent Mental Health Services – would ultimately decide if Sam really was autistic, and if so, what level of help he would need. The ELAC team would then decide which school he could be enrolled with and, finally, social services would then update Sam's care plan to show how we, as a family, could best address and support his needs.

In the meantime, as a family, there was some nice news. In the form of an invitation from my niece Chloe – my sister Donna's daughter – to a wedding just under six weeks hence. Closely followed (*Six weeks away? Whattt?* had been my first thought) by a call from Donna herself.

'Sorry,' she said immediately. 'I meant to call you last week. But it's all been so manic since I saw you –'

'I'm not surprised!' I interrupted. 'What's going on? Why? I thought they were getting married *next* spring, not *this* spring.'

'D'oh,' my sister laughed. 'Because she's just found out she's pregnant!'

'*Really?*' I said. 'Wow. That's certainly … unexpected.' And it was. My niece was the last person on earth I'd have expected to be expecting unexpectedly. Just like her mum she had life organised to the nth degree. Yes, she'd been with her fiancé a good while now, and they were definitely planning to have children, but as far as I'd been aware, they'd planned to do things in a slightly different order to the one my sister sketched out to me now.

'Oh, they hummed and hawed about it,' she explained. 'They initially thought they'd just have the baby and get married next year, like they'd planned to, but in the end she decided she'd rather be a bride without a baby, in preference to being in the first throes of motherhood – fat and tired, as she put it, bless her – and as it's turned out they can have a venue *gratis*, it was a no-brainer.'

Donna went on to explain that Jack's boss – Jack being Chloe's fiancé, and a chef – had offered them the use of the marquee at his hotel, after they'd had a late cancellation. And though Donna sympathised with the girl who'd cancelled – as did I, poor thing, because her fiancé had apparently split up with her – she also saw it as fate making the decision for them. 'They'll save shedloads. Which they'll need, of course. So, can you make it?'

I could hear the excitement in my sister's voice, like a fizz down the phone line. Not only was she about to plunge into full mother-of-the-bride mode, she was also going to have her greatest wish granted and become a grandmother like I was, to boot. And there was to be another baby in the family, which always made me happy.

So my first response would normally have been *just try to keep me away*. Which is exactly what I said. But with a caveat: Sam. Chloe and her fiancé lived a hundred and fifty miles away now and though I was fairly sure Mike could organise a couple of days off, we'd also need to organise respite. It was almost certain that my own kids and their respective entourages would be going (turning up to the opening of an envelope was a Watson family trait) and only the other day Christine Bolton had been telling me that the service was almost at breaking point, with respite carers currently so thin on the ground that they were having to go further and further afield to find any – perhaps as far away as where Chloe lived? Conceivably.

'So just bring him with you,' was Donna's immediate response when I told her. Which was so like her. Come one, come all. And that despite his little episode in her café. But then she didn't know Sam *that* well, did she?

'Absolutely not,' was Mike's, an hour later, when I told *him*.

And he was resolute. We had a right to a couple of days off. We'd forgone a planned trip to take on Sam in the first place, so it was a problem we had to be extremely firm about – as in placing it very firmly on social services' shoulders. 'It's not fair, love,' he'd added, seeing the doubt in my face. 'Yes, you've made strides with Sam – big strides – but things are still far from perfect, and who knows how he'll react in the company of complete strangers? And it's not fair on you to have the stress of looking after him all day and evening. And what if he has one of his meltdowns during the service? That's definitely not fair on Chloe.'

He had a point. A very good point. It was Chloe's day and it wouldn't be right to potentially disrupt it just because *we* had a problem. So I'd just have to put my foot down. And though a part of me still thought we could cross that bridge when we came to it, only a couple of days later I had further evidence that perhaps we couldn't. That I'd been lulled into a false sense of security.

In fact, it was in the night-time when it happened – at 3.20 in the morning. A horrible time to be jolted awake at the best of times, but even worse when you were woken by screaming. And there was something about Sam's screams that never failed to go right through me.

'I'll go,' I whispered to Mike, who had also woken up. 'You go back to sleep, love. You've got to be up in three hours.'

'Wha? Wha time is it?' he mumbled as I pushed the covers back. Then he grunted and pulled the duvet back over his head.

Screams still piercing the silence, I pattered out onto the landing, pulling on my dressing gown as I went. I knew Tyler wouldn't wake up, at least – he'd been football training after college and it would take an earthquake to wake him after that. He might even still be wearing head-phones while sleeping – it wouldn't be the first time, as he often finished the evening with a late-night comedy podcast; it always made us smile to hear him tittering away to himself.

Sam, though, despite my assumption he was screaming in his sleep, appeared to be wide, wide awake. He was sitting bolt upright in his bed, clutching the covers under his chin, his little hands balled into tight, white fists.

But as I approached I wasn't sure he was awake after all. His face was wet from sobbing, his eyes and pupils huge, but he didn't seem to see me.

I sat down on the bed. 'Sweetheart, did you have a bad dream?' I stroked his hair as I spoke, which was damp and clinging to his forehead. 'Have you had a nasty nightmare?'

Sam nodded – so he was awake, at least half-awake – but he still stared straight ahead towards the mirror on his dressing table. I followed his line of sight and wondered fleetingly if that might be the problem. It was probably a scary thing if you woke in the night and saw a reflection of yourself in a mirror. I didn't have time to dwell on that, however, as Sam had by now begun rambling. Not quite sense – more a string of random words and phrases, only a few of which I could pick out. Dog cage. The bad man. It hurts. Mustn't tell.

Sam was beginning to shake now, as well, so I put my arm around him and gently rocked him, holding him tight but not too tight as he continued spewing words out. I still wasn't entirely sure if he was asleep or awake. The bad man. Mustn't tell. *Mustn't* tell Mummy. Courtney. He was sobbing too, little whimpers. Like a dreaming dog, chasing rabbits in its sleep.

'The bad man,' I said eventually, keeping my voice to a whisper.

'He's so *bad*,' he said immediately, and I felt him stiffen in my embrace.

'The bad man in your dream?' I tried.

He stiffened further, and tipped his face up so he could see me. I looked into frightened eyes and I realised he *was* awake. Just gripped by something – an overwhelming mental image? A memory? I'd seen similar things before in deeply distressed children – a kind of tipping point, when whatever it is that they've locked away so carefully comes tumbling out of them finally, too big to contain.

'He's *real*,' Sam said finally. 'He's proper. He's *real*.'

'And he hurt you?'

A small nod.

'In what way, sweetie?'

'My winkie. He said he wouldn't but he did! He's a *liar*!'

Can a heart 'sink'? Of course not. It's too firmly anchored. But the expression is a common one for good reason. Nothing else captures that sensation of resigned, heavy gloom quite so accurately. That moment when a person sees or hears something so wretchedly unwelcome that an exhalation or a head shake just isn't enough. His winkie. A bad man. A man who hurt his winkie. It was a Pandora's box I'd had the misfortune to have opened more than once – those few words so often the portal to a whole raft of nasties, the implications of them so huge. Were I given to swearing, I'd have sworn then, no question. *This* again.

He was crying harder now, as if the admission had opened a sluice. 'Oh, sweetheart,' I said, clutching him tighter. 'Shhh, now. It's okay. You're safe, no one can hurt you here, I promise.'

And, of course, he was. At least from the bad man who'd hurt him, whoever he was. But from the demons lodged in his head, not at all.

I riffled through mental file cards as I continued to rock him. Sexual abuse. That flipping dog cage. Not being able to tell his mummy. I knew what it meant, obviously – some sort of sexual assault. But what did it all *mean*, in terms of the role it had played in his past? Had this been an isolated incident or had it been an ongoing horror? I thought back to the few snippets I'd been learning from Christine Bolton. Sam's mother had been painted as sick and neglectful. The next-door neighbour had reported a string of men in and out of the house. I knew that alcohol, or possibly drugs, had been mentioned. Had Sam been abused by one of his mother's boyfriends? Had he been locked up in a dog cage to get him out of the way? Were both these things going on on a regular basis? It was all too easy to form a picture, because this was the stuff of my own nightmares – their foundations built on the disclosures of many children before Sam. Of being variously abused – physically, psychologically and sexually. Of being grievously neglected, of being 'used' in payment for drugs, of being treated as a sexual plaything by adult relations, of being forced to participate in horrendous, deviant acts. No, I hadn't seen it all – not yet, at least – but it sometimes felt as though I'd heard it all. And all of it coming down to the same distressing business of vulnerable children being horribly treated and defiled.

But what were the particulars here? What was Sam's particular story? I shelved the question, though. This wasn't the time or place to ask him.

'Your mummy,' I said instead, 'why didn't you feel you could tell your mummy?'

'Because he said if I did he would take me away. And never bring me back again. Not never!'

I kissed the top of his head and sighed inside. So far, so familiar. Fear was such a reliably effective holder of children's tongues.

'But you're safe now,' I said again, glancing at the time on the wall clock. 'You know that, Sam, don't you? That there's no need to be scared, because the bad man can't hurt you. Now, how about I sing you a lullaby to help you get back to sleep?'

He was limp in my arms now – probably exhausted by his turbulent awakening – so I knew it wouldn't be long before his eyes closed and he slept again.

And it wasn't. In a matter of minutes, his breathing had changed, and I was able to lie him back down and tuck the covers in around him.

Needless to say, though, I didn't get another wink.

Chapter 11

The next day I got up feeling predictably groggy, having spent the rest of the night hours awake with my thoughts. But coffee helped, as did my feeling of conviction that I would get to the bottom of Sam's disclosures. For these were key, surely, to much of his emotional distress. So, at some point during the day, I would commit them both to my log and to email, and hopefully add weight to the case for prompt action. In the meantime, however, I must let Sam lead the way.

So I got him up as normal, saw to it that he did his daily morning tasks, ticked them off his chart with lots of praise and made him breakfast. Of course, if Sam had wanted to talk about it more, I would have certainly encouraged him, but he made no reference to his nightmare, let alone its contents – as I was coming to understand was normal practice for him. Once a thing had been put out there, it was treated as done – simply parked in a mental corner and forgotten. At least for now.

I did, however, feel it appropriate to register that he'd *had* a nightmare. 'You feeling okay this morning, love?' I asked him as we ate our scrambled eggs together. 'Did you manage to sleep alright after your bad dream?'

Sam picked up his glass of orange juice and took a big slurp from it. 'I feel fine,' he said brightly, as he put it back down again. 'Am I allowed to take Flame for a walk now my jobs are done? I'm excited to do the park bit on my own again.'

I'd gone out on a slight limb over the past couple of days and, so far, it was appearing to pay dividends. Whether he'd wanted to appear grown-up or just wanted to have time with the dog alone, he'd told me a few days previously that I didn't need to go to the park with him if I was busy. That I could go home and do my 'scrubbing and stuff' while he walked Flame by himself.

I'd do no such thing, of course, not at this early stage, but I saw no harm in giving him the space to be on his own with the dog, so for the last couple of mornings we'd picked up Flame from Mrs Pegg's, and walked together to the gate to the park. There I'd left him, promising to be back at the gate in thirty minutes (I'd even given him one of Mike's old watches to wear for the purpose) and while he took a turn around the park, I had loitered with intent – intent on not being spotted while I passed the time strolling around and catching up with my friends and family on social media.

I hadn't minded. I'd read something only recently about the importance of daylight as an aid to restful sleep, and, trapped as I was currently by the needs of my caring responsibilities, a chance to be out and about every morning, for a dose of light and vitamin D, seemed like a win–win situation.

Plus, letting Sam apparently take charge of Flame (with Mrs Pegg's agreement, obviously) gave him a sense of self-esteem-boosting responsibility – something I suspected had been sorely lacking in his life up to now. And, though I hung around, I wasn't unduly concerned for his safety – the park was invariably bristling with neighbours who knew me – and Sam, too, now – dogs being such great social lubricators.

And today I'd use the time to call Colin and Christine, and give them a heads-up on the email I'd be sending later.

'That's a great idea,' I said, glancing out of the kitchen window at another bright spring morning. 'And it's a lovely day for it too, isn't it?'

Sam agreed that it was, and while I cleared away the breakfast things trotted off upstairs to get his 'kit on' – the same ensemble of welly boots, jeans and hoodie that he'd worn every day for our outings, topped off by a green waterproof jacket that had once been my grandson Levi's, the pocket stuffed with enough doggy-poo bags to last a month.

And while he did so, I got my thoughts in order. I hadn't forgotten that as well as updating social services about Sam's small hours disclosures, I also had to inform them about my niece's upcoming wedding, and my need for forty-eight hours of respite care. Not the best timing, given what else I had to tell them.

But I'd at least come around to Mike's way of thinking. Convenient as it seemed to simply take Sam along with us to the wedding, it would be a very long day for a child with such a short attention span and attendant behavioural challenges. And now we had a history of abuse in the mix, that felt even more of an issue. Given that he'd already delighted us with a couple of pretty pithy expressions, who knew what else might be in there? And might also come out, should he get stressed.

And that he'd been sexually abused I was in no doubt. It might have been an isolated incident or a longer-term horror, but I was sure he'd been telling me the truth. Like most children on the spectrum, Sam struck me as essentially an honest person – because he simply didn't have the capacity to tell lies. No matter how much trouble he might get into, there hadn't been an occasion I could remember when he hadn't told the truth, at least within a very short time of being confronted about some misdemeanour. So it was now just a matter of unravelling the things he'd told me and working out who it was that had hurt him. Last night he had mentioned a bad man, so there must be one. All we had to do now was find out who that bad man was.

'Possibly a boyfriend of the mother,' Christine had suggested when I had explained everything to her after dropping Sam and Flame off at the park gate. 'Or maybe even his own father. There's nothing on file to suggest he ever visited the home – or that he was aware of Sam's existence, for that matter. It's not even clear if the three kids even had the same father. But that doesn't mean he didn't. Or that one of the other's fathers didn't. You never know with these things, do you?'

'That's half the trouble,' I said. 'We know practically nothing about this family and their past. Are you in touch with the other siblings and their carer? I wonder if they've said anything similar.'

'I'm not personally involved with Will and Courtney,' Christine said, 'but I do know their social worker and, according to her, they're thriving in their new setting. Both in school again, both quite settled and happy. And if they'd made any disclosures about abuse she would obviously have told me.'

This saddened me. I knew I should be happy that the two little ones were settling well into their new lives. And I was, of course. How could I not be? But at the same time I was sad that poor Sam didn't have this. Yes, he was trundling along, and, increasingly, at least having more good days than bad days – especially now he had access to dogs – but there was no question that his autism presented challenges they didn't have, and to have all this on top felt like another of life's unfairnesses. Because the bottom line was another of life's uncomfortable truths: it was highly possible that he'd been the child marked out for abuse precisely *because* of his communication problems. I recalled something else Christine had told me in one of her emails. That he hadn't really started speaking properly till he was around five years old. If this was true, it was a factor that could certainly have contributed to his rages and deep unhappiness at times; it's hard not to get angry when you feel you can't properly articulate your needs.

And, depressingly, it also pointed to his unique suitability for grooming. 'Why does it so often come down to this?' Christine commented, echoing my very thoughts.

I glanced across at the green expanses beyond the park gate, to the people strolling around in the sunshine, going about their daily lives. And I mused on the dark perspective my job so often gave me – of the darkness that always existed beneath the surface.

'Why indeed?' I agreed. To which neither of us had an answer. 'Well, I'll do my absolute best to get this fast-tracked,' Christine said instead. 'I'll speak to my manager as soon as I put the phone down, in fact. We need to get this made official so that an investigation can take place. Anyway,' she added, 'how about you? How are you coping with everything?'

I decided not to mention my respite requirements until we next spoke – I didn't want her to waste any of her limited time looking into that for me when there were far more important enquiries to be made. 'Just fine,' I reassured her. 'And I'll call Colin now. Get him up to speed before I email you both later.'

I did exactly that. And Colin was predictably bullish. 'You know,' he said, once I'd outlined Sam's night-time disclosures, 'there's one way we might get more immediate answers. Why don't we just go and visit the neighbour?'

'Mrs Gallagher?'

'Exactly. It was her who alerted us to the family situation, after all. And if she's been that involved with them, she might have seen stuff that could give us some clues, mightn't she?'

'Wouldn't someone have already interviewed her?'

'I highly doubt it,' he said immediately. 'It would have hardly been a priority, after all. Not now the children have been removed to a place of safety and the mum's in hospital getting treatment. Why would they? It would only become a factor if charges end up being made against her, wouldn't it? And right now, as far as I know, that's not on the table. But this changes everything, doesn't it? And if anyone knows about the comings and goings in that household, my money is on her.'

'That's a brilliant idea,' I said. 'We could ask her all sorts and, like you said, if anyone knows, it'll be her. Assuming she'll talk to us. Do you think she'll see us?'

'I don't see why she wouldn't,' Colin said, 'though we'll obviously have to tread carefully. Confidentiality is key, so we can't mention Sam's disclosures to her – at least not at this stage. So we'll have to be careful about what we ask or say.'

I felt a bloom of positivity. I knew the cogs in social services turned slowly, and this could help no end, if it happened. It was also right up my street – a bit of private detective work? Bring it on. 'Oh, of course,' I said, 'we could just, you know, play it as a catch-up visit. Say we are trying to build up a solid background for Sam's benefit, and that we just need a kind of picture of how they lived, and ...'

Colin laughed. Loudly. He clearly had my measure. 'Easy there, Columbo,' he said. 'Give me a day or two to run it all by my manager and work out what we need. In the meantime, do you need me to come out for a visit? Take Sam off your hands for a couple of hours or something?'

I had a million ants in my pants by now, and wanted to go and see Mrs Gallagher immediately, so the thought that it might be a while away dampened my excitement somewhat. 'Oh, I see,' I said. 'Well, okay. If you think it might be a while before we can go, then, yes, I imagine that Sam would love to see you in the meantime, and of course it would give me a bit of a break. When were you thinking?'

'Couple of days? Where are we now ... let me see ... how about Thursday? Around ten? And now I'd better fly. If I hear anything in the meantime I'll call you, but, if not, I'll see you then. Oh, and best not to mention any of this to Sam yet. If at all. Or am I teaching my grandmother to suck eggs?'

I obviously chided him about the 'gran' bit, but he was right in his assessment. Sam might really miss Mrs Gallagher and, if I told him, he might want to come along as well, which obviously couldn't happen as it would potentially stop her from opening up to us. So when I ended the call and headed into the park to meet Sam I was already decided. If we could pull off a meeting it would be strictly between me and Colin.

Sam was pink-cheeked from running around and throwing balls for Flame to catch. And, as had become the norm now, full of chatter about the fun they'd had together. 'I've decided,' he said breathlessly, as he clipped on Flame's lead, 'when I'm sixteen, I'm going to live in a big, golden castle on a hill. I'm going to have a dog just like Flame. I might even call him Flame, actually. And he's going to protect me from all the bad men who live in the woods.'

'They don't sound like very nice woods,' I observed.

'Because they're proper woods. Not like *these* woods. They're *forests*. Big bad forests.'

And as I digested this imaginative foray – the curious light and shade of it – I thought *no*. Because this little conversation was, in itself, enough to convince me that I had to push this. I had to find out who had hurt this little boy, and then do my very best to try to repair the damage that had been inflicted on him.

In the here and now, in the real world, *I* would be Sam's Flame.

Chapter 12

As promised, Colin called to take Sam out the following Thursday. And, to my delight, for almost double the couple of hours he'd first proposed. They'd first gone down to the park to walk Flame, then, having returned her, back again to play football. They then headed on into town, where they'd had a mooch round a couple of shops (the games shop and the toy shop – he'd returned to me bearing Lego) after which they'd had lunch at the local burger joint.

I'd spent the time productively, of course, in the best way I knew how – by tackling a job I'd been meaning to get around to for a while now, attaching a few dozen buttons (I'd ordered a job-lot on the internet) to several shirts and a couple of blouses. It was a tedious task – made all the harder by my ropey supermarket reading glasses – but was at least improved by the soundtrack of golden oldies from my trusty radio.

And there was also news to sing about on their return. While Sam was out of earshot in the downstairs loo, Colin waggled his mobile at me. 'Just checked my emails,' he told me. 'The visit to Mrs Gallagher has been approved.'

He had other news too, which he was quick to sketch out before Sam returned to us. 'He's opened up to me a little more about what he told you.'

'Really?' I said, pleased to hear this. 'How come? In what way?'

'We were in the games shop,' he said. 'And he was enthusing about some creepy-looking computer game or other, so I took it as an opportunity to mention that I knew he'd been having nightmares. I told him I knew because you had to report things like nightmares, so we could all plan together how best we could help him with them.'

'And he was okay with that?'

'Absolutely. In fact, he took me aback a bit, to be honest, because he just came out and told me he had nightmares because of all the bad things in his head – about the bad man who used to hurt him. Just like that.'

'That's encouraging. And?'

'That was it, I'm afraid. When I asked him what they were he said he wasn't allowed to say. So I left it at that. But it's a positive that we got that far, isn't it?'

I agreed that it was. And it made the visit to see Mrs Gallagher feel even more positive. Sam had now opened up, albeit it only a little, to both me and his social worker. Mrs Gallagher had known him well. They'd had an ongoing relationship. Was there a chance that he'd opened up to her too?

Which meant the day of the visit couldn't come soon enough. And when it did (I'd roped in Kieron – and, of course, Luna – to babysit, after dropping Dee Dee at school), I was like a cat on the proverbial hot tin roof.

I'd been surprised at how well Sam had taken the news that I had to go out for a meeting, and that Kieron would be looking after him for a few hours. After all, this was another bit of new territory for him. But watching him at the window, looking out for my son's arrival, I realised he was quite looking forward to it.

'When is he going to get here?' he whined. 'He's taking *ages*. We're going to go hunting,' he added. 'We're going to hunt for old tennis balls.'

'Are you really?'

'And we might take a picnic. *And* some dog biscuits. To reward them. Shall I get my gear on?'

'Not just yet, sweetie. I imagine he'll want to stop for a cup of coffee before you go on your adventure.'

Sam's expression darkened. 'But it's too long!' he declared with a huff. A huff that could so easily turn into a puff, and then a rage, and a full-on blow-the-house-down scenario. 'Now, now,' I said firmly. 'Remember what we've said? About being a big boy and waiting for people to be ready to do things first? Without getting angry about why you might have to wait a little bit?'

The moment passed. And I was pleased. We really were making strides with him. 'I'll be a good boy,' he said. 'I want my good-boy stars, don't I? Can we say ten minutes? That's a *long* time. But I promise I won't get angry.'

'Let's say fifteen,' I countered, smiling. 'I think fifteen will be long enough.' But, in the event, when Kieron got to us, it took no more than five, because Luna, seeing Sam, bounced around like a mad thing, and Kieron was similarly anxious to get her to the park before she did the unforgiveable and peed on my carpet.

Which meant that they were long gone by the time Colin arrived to pick me up. And he too seemed in particularly high spirits. So much so that I suspected I'd met a kindred one in him.

'So they're looking at all outcomes,' Colin explained, when we set off and I asked him about the education situation. 'It all rests on the results of the assessment, of course – which is happening as soon as humanly possible, I promise – but we're covering the bases in advance, so we're ready. We've got one person contacting all the special schools, and another all the mainstream ones. Well, at least those that have a decent SENs department, obviously. That way, all the groundwork will have already been done and we can get him in somewhere as soon as we get a diagnosis.'

'That's brilliant,' I said, 'and it will be so good for him to be back in school. It must be so boring for such a young lad to be stuck at home with a pair of oldies like me and Mike.'

Colin laughed. 'I never said that,' he pointed out, throwing his car around yet another corner, while I resisted the urge to grab the door handle. Hmm, I thought. He might not have said it but I definitely felt it.

I'd not been so traumatised since I'd rashly agreed to take Kieron out for practice while he'd been having driving lessons. An experience I knew I'd be (reluctantly) repeating with Tyler too, before too long. Still, Colin's energy was invigorating and, not for the first time, I felt glad to be in the presence of such an example of can-do youth. If anyone could clear a path to Sam's future, I reckoned Colin could. 'Ah,' he added, as we entered a lengthy street of terraced houses, 'it looks as though we're heading into the estate now, doesn't it?'

I followed his gaze up the street, feeling the usual fluttering of butterflies in my stomach. There had been a number of occasions over the years when I'd been required to enter the 'lion's den', and it was always accompanied by the same frisson of nervous anticipation. Which wasn't to say that I was generally expecting actual lions, obviously, but there was still that moment, when it happened, where I came face-to-face with a child's past – a past that, up to that point, I had only read and heard about. And, given the kind of children that Mike and I were often asked to take in, it wasn't unusual to find that it wasn't a pretty place. So whatever I was about to be faced with on the surface, I was already primed to expect that when we peeled back the layers there would be a sorry story of some kind underneath.

This estate, on the far side of town, looked fairly typical. Dense with houses, but not garages. These homes had been built decades ago, by the look of them, when few working-class people had cars. No longer. It now had cars running along the length of each kerb, despite it being in the middle of a weekday. It was also, with the odd, very obvious exception, unloved; several of the gardens had missing fences, there was rubbish lying around all over, and lots of wheelie bins – dragged out, presumably for emptying – which were overflowing with yet more rubbish, along with satellite bin bags, some already broken into by the birds. I could hear dogs barking, lots of them – aimless canine conversation – and though I'm as far from being a snob as you could possibly be, the whole area screamed poverty and hopelessness and tired, unfulfilled lives, and that made me very sad indeed.

'Bit grim round here, isn't it?' Colin said. Had he read my thoughts? Probably not, I decided. We worked in the same ball park, so he didn't really need to. He probably spent more time going to houses in streets like this than me. He then glanced at the sat nav, which was telling him to turn right. 'I think Mrs Gallagher's is just around this next corner.'

He took this one more slowly, of necessity – there wasn't much room for manoeuvre – and we both let out an 'ahh' together.

'This looks a bit nicer,' he said as we took in the change. This was obviously a street where a few houses had been sold off a while back, because, in contrast to the ones we'd just passed, some had that unmistakeable look of private ownership. They were semis on this street, with bigger front gardens, and, though still modest, several were definitely better taken care of. Fresh paint, replacement windows, shrubs and flowers. I noted the park across the road. Perhaps that made them more desirable.

And, it turned out, perhaps not unsurprisingly, that Mrs Gallagher's was even more spruced up than most. We pulled up outside to see a lush, green and neatly mown lawn, bordered on two sides by the last remnants of a display of spring daffodils, with tulips thrusting up like red-bereted soldiers in between. There were gleaming white nets hanging from all the front windows and the front door – painted blue – had a brass knocker attached to it that was the size of a tea plate.

'Well, this definitely looks nicer,' I said, as I climbed out of the car. I looked to the houses left and right, both of which were outshone by Mrs Gallagher's. 'I wonder which one was Sam's?'

'Looks like we're about to find out,' Colin said, nodding across the roof of the car towards the front door. I followed his glance to see a lady was already emerging from it; she looked around sixty and was smiling and waving at us.

'You must be from the social,' she said as we walked up the path towards her. She had a soft Irish accent and curly, steel-coloured hair. 'Ah, come along inside and we'll all have a nice cup of tea. Though would you mind if I asked you to leave your shoes in the hallway? We don't stand on ceremony here, but I do like my carpets clean.'

A woman after my own heart, then, I thought, as we did as instructed. And small too – unusually, she was almost as small as me. She was also wearing a garment I'd not seen in a while – one of those sleeved, wraparound aprons my gran used to don to do her housework. There was also a string of pearls around her neck.

The house interior was just as well-kept as the exterior. Every window ledge, every cabinet, every ornament and photograph-covered surface – of which there were a lot.

'Your home is lovely,' I said, as she showed us into a conservatory behind the rear sitting room, where a tray of tea things was already waiting on the cloth-covered table. 'Though I have to say, it must take forever to dust.'

'Oh, it does that,' she trilled, 'but I do love my dusting. My mother was a proud woman,' she added, 'and she'd turn in her grave, she would, if I didn't keep my home absolutely spotless. Now then, make yourselves at home, while I go and fetch the tea.'

'At *home*? I'm not sure I dare twitch, let alone move,' Colin whispered with a wink as she trotted off. 'Jeez – she could clean up on *Flog It!*, no question.'

He was right. Or *Antiques Roadshow*, for that matter. I was still grinning when Mrs Gallagher returned, with the promised pot of tea and a plate of what looked like freshly baked fairy cakes. 'We're all of us the same in our part of the world,' she went on, as if still midway through our conversation. 'I'm from County Sligo,' she added, as if this fact was key. 'All the women there were the same. Oh, they would judge each other to be the Devil himself if the house didn't smell of furniture polish and disinfectant. Now, in case you're wondering,' she said, nodding towards the fence bordering one of the adjacent houses, 'over there's where the hussy and her little ones lived. You only need to take a look at those mucky windows to know it was a house of sin.'

It was difficult to see next door's windows because the conservatory had Venetian blinds, but no doubt the muckiness of them would become clear eventually.

'Anyway,' Mrs Gallagher said, making the sign of the cross across her chest as she set down the teapot. 'We'll leave that to brew a while, will we? So. What would you like to know?'

Colin sat forward a little, so I left him to lead the way. 'Anything you can help us with, Mrs Gallagher,' he said as she took her own seat. 'Anything that might help us form a better picture of Sam's home life. I understand that Mrs Gough suffered from mental health problems. You've known the family a good while, I'm told, so did she always struggle with the kids, or was it just more recently?'

Mrs Gallagher puffed her chest out. 'Mental health, my backside!' she said, suddenly as sharp as the pots of cacti that sat on her conservatory windowsills. 'I'd have assumed you'd have known that much. Pardon my French, but the woman was a fecking horror. Never a good word for those wee ones, not a one. Cold-hearted, she was, and the men she had! Oh, I can tell you, I lost count of the comings and goings long ago. Didn't care what age they were either. Young ones, old ones, she didn't care which. As long as she could palm those children off with me, she was happy. Mental health? No bloody backbone more like. Unless that's a fancy term for being drunk as a lord on a daily basis.'

My gaze landed on a crucifix hung in one of the alcoves back in the sitting room. The term 'judge not lest you be judged' came to mind. I was stunned, to say the least, at her uncompromising, brutal honesty, and, from the set of his shoulders, guessed Colin was too. But we'd come for some insight, and insight this was. She clearly had not a jot of sympathy for her neighbour.

'I see,' Colin said, as Mrs Gallagher poured the tea. It was teak coloured, steaming. Not my cup of tea at all. But perhaps she thought coffee was the work of the Devil too. I certainly wouldn't have dreamt of asking for some.

'Oh, I've seen it all,' Mrs Gallagher said, warming to her theme. 'Forgive me for speaking out, but it's been *such* a long time coming. Please do have a cake. They're gluten-free. I'm a martyr to my stomach, sad to say.'

Colin duly took one. But I demurred, patting my own stomach as justification. And while he bit into it, I asked the question I'd burned to ask since we'd arrived here. 'Tell me,' I said, 'little Sam's mentioned a dog cage, more than once. A place he used to go into … And there's been talk of him apparently being locked in there. Do you know anything about that? It's been quite an ongoing thing with him.'

'Oh, indeed I do,' she said. 'And yes, you're quite right. I tell you what, why don't you both come upstairs with me? I can even show it to you then.' She got up. Colin put his tea and half the cake down. 'Come along, then you'll be able to see it for yourselves.'

We duly followed her back into the hall and trooped up the stairs, past the watching eyes of what were presumably various relatives, whose images were behind glass on the staircase wall. 'He was in there all the time,' she said as she led us up. 'I've no proof but then I don't really need any. It was common knowledge that she locked him in there when she wanted a bit of peace. And, well, you'll know he has his problems ... Going off on one the way he does ... Has he howled?' she added, turning back to me as she reached the landing. 'Such a fearful, fearful noise. It's a wonder she held on to them as long as she did. It was a racket that could wake up the dead, let alone the social.'

'Yes, he has,' I said, as we crammed next to the window on the tiny landing.

'Poor mite,' Mrs Gallagher said, as she swept aside the net. 'Hours at a time he'd be in there. And in all weathers, too.'

We peered down, and Mrs Gallagher's garden was revealed. And, beyond the fence, in the garden beyond it there was indeed a dog cage, sited at the end, and therefore in plain view of both this, and, presumably, the far neighbour's upstairs windows. It was in two parts; a wooden kennel – quite a large one – with a caged area attached; a lockable enclosure that presumably formed a dog run. So this was the place Sam had talked about.

'And there was a dog?' Colin asked. 'Sam's mentioned having had a dog once.'

'Oh, it pre-dates the Goughs,' Mrs Gallagher explained. 'The man who lived here before him had a pair of grey-hounds. But yes, the Goughs did have a dog, briefly. Well, a puppy. They didn't have it long before it got out and got run over. The woman couldn't even find the wherewithal to keep a *dog* alive.' Her tone was bitter. 'Since then *that* thing has just sat out there, rotting.'

Another sadness, I thought. But Mrs Gallagher tutted. 'Look at it,' she said. 'No place to bring kids up, is it? Look at the muck and mess down there. More like a tip than a garden. It's a wonder one of those little ones didn't end up in hospital.'

We both looked, as she suggested, and Colin and I exchanged glances. She was right. On the face of it, it *was* no place to bring kids up; choked with triffid-like weeds, full of junk, broken toys and bits of furniture, and bags of rubbish. The house also looked unlived in, because probably it was now. And would presumably stay that way till decisions were made about Sam's mother's future. If she wasn't going back there, it would presumably be rented out to a new family. I wondered if it still contained things of Sam's that he might be missing. Though as he hadn't said, I doubted it. I doubted they'd had very much.

I wondered about Mrs Gallagher's forbearance in not reporting the family to social services before she had. Or had she? Had she acted on her fears and got nowhere? Or had she initially taken the view that it was none of her business how her neighbour had decided to live her life?

'You say you looked after the children a lot?' I asked as she lowered the curtain again and swept a hand across the sill. I knew the action well. Reconnaissance, in the perennial war against dust.

'Oh, they were around here all the time,' she said, her expression softening at the memory. 'Dear little things. Loved to come and play here. All of them, Sam included. Oh, I know he wasn't the easiest of children, but that's not the point, is it? You get what God gives you and you do your very best with them. Your *very* best,' she said again, as she led us back down the stairs.

We followed and this time I looked properly at the photos we were passing. There were several of a little boy, around Sam's age, but not Sam. 'Who's this?' I asked as we reached the bottom most. 'What a lovely-looking little boy.'

Mrs Gallagher stopped, smiling fondly, then straightened the picture very slightly. Imperceptibly, to my eye. It had looked straight already. Her action seemed much more like a loving ritual. 'Oh, that's my Seany,' she said. 'A little stunner he was, wasn't he? I dare say he'd have broken a few hearts, given half a chance. Spit of his dad, he was as a lad. Everyone used to say so.' She sighed heavily and I sensed I'd stumbled on something very painful.

'He has the most beautiful eyes,' I added, when she didn't add anything further.

'Piercing,' she said finally. 'Aren't they? The kind that folks used to say could see right into your soul. And they were right. Anyway,' she finished, clearing her throat noisily, 'that tea will be going cold. Come back on in.'

'Oh God, do you think he died?' I asked Colin once we were back in the car and safely out of earshot.

'I thought exactly the same thing,' Colin said, as he flipped down the indicator and pulled out into the road. 'Or maybe her husband did. No evidence of one being around, was there? Maybe someone at the office will know. But she clearly didn't want to talk about it, did she? So perhaps her son *is* dead.'

'That's so *sad*,' I said. 'The poor woman. I feel really bad now.'

'Why bad?' Colin wanted to know. 'You didn't do anything wrong.'

'Bad for *her*,' I clarified.

'Ah,' he said. 'Of course.' He was silent for a moment – musing thoughtfully on life's lottery, just as I was? – before glancing across at me. 'Anyway – Sam. We didn't learn a great deal, did we?'

I shook my head as I clicked my seat belt. 'I know, but sometimes it's the things that aren't said that reveal the most. I was just thinking – if she's on her own, and has lost her own son – well, that speaks volumes, doesn't it? She must have looked at the way those kids were being treated by their mother and it must have burned into her soul. You know – the unfairness of it all. Maybe that's why she was so prickly about her. So unsympathetic.'

'She was certainly that, wasn't she?' Colin said. 'Borderline harsh, I thought. Not much empathy. And you're right – that does speak volumes, and might well be because she lost her own son, and feels bitter about her neighbour having three and treating them so badly. She might not have said anything incriminating but she was pretty clear that the whole mental illness thing doesn't wash with her, wasn't she? I mean, Sam's mother is currently in an expensive mental health facility, so we have to assume *they* think she's mentally ill, but Mrs Gallagher clearly doesn't. Or even if she does have mental health issues, she obviously thinks they're self-inflicted. The legacy of a party lifestyle that definitely didn't include her kids.'

'And the abuser could so easily have been a boyfriend, couldn't it?' I mused. 'It would hardly be front-page news, would it?'

'Exactly,' said Colin. 'Far from it. But at least we have confirmation that there were different men coming in and out of Sam's life. Which will add weight to what he's disclosed to you, won't it?'

Which it would. Which was important – because I knew that things weren't cut and dried, and that Sam would be believed wasn't a given. Though, in truth, Mrs Gallagher hadn't really told us anything I hadn't already worked out for myself, other than her fierce attachment to the children whose apparently chaotic lives she'd watched being played out on the other side of the garden fence.

And it did look chaotic. No wonder Sam struggled so much with normality. Had he ever known 'normal'? Was that why he was always so busy building things with Lego, only to smash them down again? Perhaps that was all he had ever known.

Chapter 13

Though the visit to Mrs Gallagher hadn't revealed as much as I'd hoped, it had, at least, painted more of a picture. Not a nice picture, obviously, and it was still light on detail, but at least I had an image in my head to refer to, and confirmation that Sam had suffered long-term abuse.

Abuse takes many forms, of course, as do abusers, and I was mindful that it helped no one to do that knee-jerk thing of casting Sam's mother as a villain. I knew nothing of her own background and it was possible, even likely, that she was a victim herself. Be it of her own damaged childhood, or drugs, or whatever, I still subscribed to the view that humans were rarely born evil – rather more often than not, they did bad things as a result of having bad things done to them in the first place – and so the cycle continued in perpetuity.

Our job now – mine, social services, the carers looking after Sam's siblings – was to do our level best to stop the rot. And, the obvious neglect aside, the priority for Sam was to get to the root of his demons. If we could do that (so went the theory, anyway), we could help him address them and deal with them, giving him the best chance to go on to live a happy life.

And, while we continued with the socialising and self-control bit – using the chart, which seemed to be helping – this meant investigating his disclosures of sexual abuse.

So I was pleased, just a couple of days after our visit to Mrs Gallagher's, to get a call on that very subject from Christine Bolton.

'I'm sorry you've had it so tough, Casey,' she started off. 'I know it's hard waiting around in the background for news, but I'm happy to report that we are at last making progress. I'm in a position to organise an interview so we can follow up on Sam's recent disclosures.'

'That's good news,' I said.

'Indeed it is,' Christine said, 'though, as always, we have to tread carefully. And that's especially true in Sam's case, given his young age and limited capacity for understanding. So we've opted for the local family centre.'

Christine went on to explain that a plain-clothed CID officer would meet us – Sam, Colin and myself – at the family centre close to where we lived. I'd been there before, of course, so I knew it well; it was a place with a variety of uses, including planning meetings, and contact between children in care and their relatives – so they could be conducted in a safe, neutral space. It was also the place where delicate meetings, such as the one arranged for Sam happened; where they could be sensitively, but also officially probed, about potentially actionable disclosures they'd made. The officer, a female, would use a variety of techniques to get Sam to open up and talk about the abuse.

Well, at least in theory. In my experience, despite the deliberately homely nature of the venue, such interviews often proved tricky. Faced with a stranger, however well-trained and well-meaning, children would often clam up from fear. But Sam had already mentioned the 'bad man' to Colin as well as me, so perhaps we could dare to hope he wouldn't – especially if both of us were there to support him.

But that wasn't the biggest potential problem. 'At that stage, if Sam is comfortable,' Christine went on, 'Colin may be asked to wait in another room – and perhaps you too; the officer will tell you – and then, obviously depending on the outcome of the chat, she will decide how, or if, to proceed.'

That 'if' wasn't unexpected. Nor were Christine's next words, as she described how she'd already spoken to the CID officer, and how, at the moment, they wouldn't be discounting the possibility that Sam, like other children of his age and background, might have invented the 'bad man' as a way of explaining and focusing his hurt. How badly would it affect him, if, having spoken out, his testimony was dismissed as lies?

On the other hand, if Sam *was* believed it would be equally traumatic. Better in the long term, of course – and not just for Sam, but because justice would be done – but in the short term, if his abuser was identified and found, it would involve him in giving even more formal testimony – being put 'through the mill' in the way the law rightly demanded. There was no escaping it – he was damned if they did and damned if they didn't.

'I know your gut feeling is strong,' Christine conceded, 'as is mine. Would that it wasn't, eh? But we now have to leave them to get on with their job, I suppose. Anyway, the main thing is that we've taken a step forward with all this. How are you fixed for next week? I have a couple of possible dates in mind. Does Tuesday work? I'm thinking the sooner the better.'

'Tuesday's fine,' I said. 'Sooner is definitely better. Oh, and while I'm on,' I added, putting my anxieties about it aside by seizing what seemed like the perfect opportunity, 'is there any chance you could find us an overnight respite carer, please? My niece Chloe is getting married in a little under a month, and all our lot will obviously be going. And it's a long way away, hence the overnight stay. I'd obviously take Sam if I could, but what with everything that's been going on, it doesn't seem sensible. I'm not sure he's quite up to that kind of thing just yet. Sorry to spring it on you. It's all been a bit short notice.'

'Of course,' Christine said, without so much as a shred of hesitation. Perhaps things weren't quite as bad as I'd feared. 'Can't have you missing a family wedding,' she went on. 'That would never do. Tell you what, email the dates to me. I'm bound to forget otherwise. Anyway, got a pen? I'll email the details of all this to you obviously, but for the moment – I have to double-check it's still okay for him, obviously – Colin will meet you at the centre at half eleven for twelve o'clock. The officer's name is Kim Dearing. Oh, and one thing she mentioned – could you try to prep Sam in advance? Well, as much as you can, obviously. She just wants to be sure he'll be prepared for what she'll be talking to him about.' Christine chuckled then. 'As if you, of all people, need telling any of this, eh? I'll bet you've done more of this sort of thing than any of us!'

Which might well be true, but, at the same time, the word 'try' was key. I might have experience of such matters, but it meant next to nothing because different children reacted to stress in all sorts of ways, and I had no idea which way Sam might go. Tuesday was still days away, so did I start prepping him now, in the hopes that he'd get used to the idea, or wait till the last minute to spare him angsty anticipation?

Having worked with children on the spectrum many times before I knew that fear of the unknown played a big part in their make-up, as did anxiety about any change to routine. So, whichever way I played it, this would probably be upsetting – it was just a coin toss as to which would prove worse. If I sprang it on him an hour before the meeting he might get so worked up he wouldn't be able to talk in any coherent manner, but if I told him today, that would give him several days to worry about meeting a stranger and sharing his hidden secrets with her.

So I decided on a halfway house of drip-feeding little bits. But casually, as if it was really no big deal. Just something not-very-important that was happening next week.

'Oh, by the way, Sam,' I said over our lunch that day, 'remember the other night when you had that bad dream?'

Sam looked immediately suspicious. 'I never counted to a hundred,' he said. 'I didn't, Casey, honest.'

I filed that snippet of peculiar information away for the time being. 'I know you didn't,' I said lightly. 'I was just talking about what. About that bad man? Anyone would have been scared about that, anyone. So, anyway, because I care about you, I told this important lady. Just so she might have some good ideas about stopping those nasty dreams from frightening you.' I touched his arm. 'Just wanted to check, really. Was that okay?'

Sam sighed – one of his theatrical ones – but then he nodded. 'I *s'pose*. But who's the special lady? Is she a doctor?'

I tipped my head, feigning thought. 'No, I don't think she's a doctor,' I said. 'Just a really clever lady with a lot of good ideas about how to help little boys who have nightmares. Anyway, we'll see what she says, eh?'

Sam took a big bite of his cheese and ham toastie and chewed. 'So, like a superhero who kills bad guys?' he asked once he'd swallowed.

'Yes, a little bit like that, I suppose,' I agreed. 'Though as far as I know she doesn't wear a cape.'

'That's cool,' he said. So, so far, so good.

The next day, which was Saturday – which meant the men in the family were all worshipping at the altar of football – we took both Flame and Luna out for an especially long walk, physical tiredness being an excellent elixir for stressy kids.

Throwing a stick for Luna (I had been converted by Sam's no-ball-doohickey laziness), I said, 'Guess what, Sam, that really clever lady I was talking about? She's called Kim, and she said she'd like to meet you. She's really excited to see if she can help you. What do you think?'

Sam threw his own stick, for Flame. 'The superhero lady?' he asked, as Flame galloped off to fetch it. 'That's cool. She sounds cool. When is she coming?'

'She's not coming. We're going. To meet *her*. Colin's coming along too.'

'Cool,' Sam said again. 'Does she live in, like, a bunker?'

I couldn't help but laugh. 'No, not a bunker. Just a house.'

'But a secret house.'

'Erm, not *exactly* …' Perhaps I'd run with this too far now. 'But it *is* a very special house.'

'How special?'

'In that it's a place where people help people. Children especially.'

'Like a safe house?'

'Er … yes, I suppose you could call it that. Anyway,' I hurried on, 'won't it be nice to see Colin? He said that afterwards, if you like, he'll take you for lunch. Do you like the sound of that?'

But Sam was still off on his own trajectory. 'So, Sampson *and* a superhero lady at the same time. That's *way* cool. You never know, they might blow up the world!'

Little man, I couldn't help but think, as I saw his excitement, *in reality, they might just blow up your world*.

And which might take a bit more rebuilding than Lego.

Chapter 14

Our local family centre was a large converted guest house. It was in a residential area, and externally it looked just like its neighbours, so if you passed it you might not even realise what it was, let alone have any notion of what, on any given day, might be going on within.

All sorts happened here, of course – some of it routine, some of it sad, or bad, or shocking – from birth parents making halting overtures to children currently in the council's care, to meetings such as this, where troubled children had a safe space to speak out. And in a place designed not to scare or overwhelm them.

The family room, into which we'd brought Sam, was the epitome of cosy. It was a room for all seasons, with a low, book-strewn table and squashy armchairs at one end, and a well-stocked play and 'chill-out' area, with Disney posters on the walls behind it, and full of toys, books, puzzles, board games and beanbags. It always reminded me of the corner I had created in my classroom, back when I was a school behaviour unit manager. There it had functioned as both a place to shut the world out, and a place to bring it in, sometimes, too – as challenged children, locked into negative behaviours, could dare to imagine the world beyond their own troubled environment.

Sam was still in anticipatory mode – part excited, part nervous – something I'd noticed from his choice of attire. He'd opted for an assemblage of favourite clothing items, including his dog-walking anorak (despite the warmth of the day), and, though he had nothing to put in it bar a carton of juice and a banana, his Spider-Man backpack. Always good to know your favourite superhero has – literally – got your back.

I had been to this type of interview before, with a number of children in our care, but as each child is different, each situation unique, you never really knew how they were going to go, so Sam's demeanour as we sat down meant nothing. I knew, both from knowing Sam and from my experience of similar encounters, that the smallest thing could send the chat off in all kinds of directions or, as sometimes happens, shut it down immediately. We started well, though. After ten minutes of 'getting to know you' time with all of us, the CID officer, Kim (to whom I gave a mental 'high five' for immediately noting the significance of the almost empty backpack), seemed to instinctively understand Sam's capacity. And, better still, seemed to have inspired his confidence. And that despite looking not a bit like a superhero. If anything, with her gentle voice and soft, unhurried manner, she looked more librarian than hard-bitten copper – though I didn't doubt she'd seen more than enough time on the streets wrangling hard-bitten criminals into submission.

But now it was time to step up a gear. And, in picking the precise moment when Sam alluded to her being a kind of superhero, she chose her moment well. 'Oh my,' she said, 'just wait till I get back to the office, Sam! Once I reveal my superpowers, I'll get the top job for sure – and at the very least, first pick when someone brings in donuts.' She then barely paused for breath before moving swiftly on to, 'Speaking of which, I think Colin needs to nip out to the shops, don't you?' Then, glancing at him only to confirm this was the moment (so I was obviously to be allowed to stay with Sam, which I was pleased about), added, 'While you and I – and Casey, of course – get on with the important superhero business of chatting about what to do about these bad dreams of yours.'

Colin stood up. 'I'd better get off then, kiddo,' he said to Sam, touching his shoulder. 'But I won't be far – or away for long. You'll be fine with that, won't you?'

'Course,' Sam said, and grinned. 'Course, Sampson. You can go.'

'Sampson?' Kim Dearing asked.

'Like the strong man,' Sam told her.

'Oh, I *see*,' she said. 'Of *course*. So, Sam, shall we start? Shall we go back to the other night, when you had the bad dream and Casey found you all upset?'

Sam glanced at me. As he would. As would most children in that scenario. My Kieron would still expect me to answer the GP's questions for him right up till the time he turned twenty.

But it wasn't for me to speak. Because that wasn't my role. Indeed, my role was clear in these situations: just to be there. I knew this well because it was part of our training. I was simply there as a reassuring presence, to help give Sam the confidence to speak out. I couldn't lead any lines of enquiry, much less answer questions for him. And though I wasn't yet sure he knew me well enough to have acquired that vital confidence, the fact that he looked at me so automatically was encouraging.

Kim had already got out a large pad – not an official-looking notebook of the kind the police usually used, but more like a child's colouring book, with balloons and clowns on the cover.

Sam eyed it. 'What's that book for?'

'It's my notebook,' Kim said simply. 'My memory is just *terrible*. I'd forget my head if it wasn't screwed on. So I make notes in here to help me remember.'

'About the bad man?'

'Among other things.'

'Are you going to shoot him for me?'

'That I'm not. Even for superheroes, shooting people is against the law. But I'd love to know who he is. What he looks like, if you can tell me? I could even draw a picture of him if you describe him to me, so we'll all know who to look out for.'

Sam shook his head emphatically. 'You can't do a picture because he's invisible when he's the bad man,' he told her.

'Invisible?'

Sam put his hands to his eyes. 'I have to wear a mask thing.'

Said so matter of factly, this shocked me to my core. Kim merely nodded. 'I see,' she said. 'That mustn't have been very nice for you. What's he like, then?'

Again, Sam answered without hesitation. 'He's like a really bad superhero, and he takes kids away.'

'Did somebody take you away?'

Sam nodded. 'Yes, a lot of times. Sometimes, once, even when I was in the dog hut. Till I made it safe.'

I filed this in my brain. 'Who put you in the dog hut, Sam?' Kim asked. 'Was it your mummy, or the bad man?'

I could feel the anxiety begin to build in Sam now. See the way he had begun twitching his leg. 'Not the bad man,' he said. 'Sometimes Mummy put me in there. She took care of me sometimes,' he added. Kim made a note.

'Sam, you told Casey that the bad man hurt you. Down below. Can you tell me anything more about that?'

Tears immediately began to pool above Sam's lower lashes. *Just like that*, I thought. *Instantaneous. It was that bad a memory*. 'I didn't like it, I didn't. He said I did, but I didn't. He said it was good but it was bad.'

Since there was nothing in the rules to stop me comforting Sam, I did. I put my arm around his shoulder and squeezed him tight for a moment. 'It's okay, sweetheart,' I whispered. 'You're doing a great job. A really great job.'

'Casey's right,' Kim said softly. 'You really are doing a great job. Was this bad man someone who your mummy knew? A boyfriend?'

Sam blinked at her, and a tear escaped to track down his cheek. 'Mummy knows him, but he was gonna kill Mummy. Or take me away. And never, ever, ever bring me back again. I had to touch his winkie as well, or he would, and I *hate* him.'

Kim leaned in towards him with her pad. 'Do you think you could tell me what the bad man looks like, Sam? When he isn't being invisible?'

Sam shook his head, almost violently, and then looked up at me, his eyes beseeching. 'I feel sick, Casey, I want to go home. I can't tell, or he'll get me, he will.'

'No one's going to get you, sweetie,' I soothed. 'I absolutely promise you.'

'That's right, Sam,' Kim said. 'You're safe here, I promise too. You say Mummy knows him. Do you know how? Was he her friend?'

'He said he was but he wasn't. He's a *liar*. And he hurt me! And I can't *tell*!'

This was escalating fast. Sam was shaking now, badly. I looked over at Kim, signalling my own anxiety. 'Would it be okay if we finished up for now?'

Kim smiled and nodded. Closed her pad. 'That's enough for now,' she agreed. 'And, you know, Sam, you've been *so* brave. Just like a superhero yourself. I think you might deserve a special lunch now. What do you think, Casey?'

'I agree,' I said, standing up and smoothing Sam's hair from his face. 'How about we go find Colin, and then go somewhere special?'

Sam nodded, clearly relieved that the questions were over. He picked up his backpack, and when I held out my hand to him, he grabbed it tighter than he ever had before.

'I need the toilet, Casey,' he whispered as we left the room. '*Badly*. Can I go here?'

'That's fine, Sam,' said Kim. 'This way.' She led us around a corner, towards the back of the house. 'The toilet is right here.'

'So what do you think?' I asked as soon as Sam was out of earshot. 'Because, if anything, I'm even more convinced he's telling the truth now.'

Kim slipped her pad under her arm. 'Not a great deal to go on, obviously. But, yes, poor little mite. For what it's worth, I do too.'

Yes.

Colin was waiting in the reception when we returned to it. And had clearly used his time productively. 'Hey, kiddo,' he said to Sam, rising from his chair and waggling his mobile. 'You fancy some fun? I know a place that has *the* most enormous play area. Ball pool and all. You ever been in a ball pool?'

'What's a ball pool?' Sam asked him. 'Is it like a swim-ming pool with balls in?'

It was heartbreaking. He was nine and he'd never seen a ball pool. 'Better than that even,' Colin said. 'It's a pool *made out of* balls. And you can kind of swim in it – and, best of all, you don't even get wet.'

This seemed sufficient to distract Sam from brooding on what had just happened. In fact, within minutes his mood had begun to bounce back, not least because, in response to his question, I assured him that for being such a good boy on our trip he'd earned a couple of extra stars today.

But perhaps it was inevitable that I had done a mental 'high five' too soon. Though, in fairness to me, at that point it felt like things were going well. When we arrived at the pub, Sam could hardly manage to get out what he wanted to eat, so desperate was he to get to the play area. And since it was a school day (we were still just under a fortnight away from the Easter holidays) I could already see he'd have free rein over it too, as only parents with pre-schoolers were in the pub.

Having found a seat close by, and taken charge of his backpack, coat and trainers, I took the opportunity to give a rundown to Colin of the gist of what Sam had said to Kim. And my confidence that she'd taken him seriously and that they were going to take things further.

'I imagine they'll probably email us with their report,' Colin said, 'so I'll make sure I forward it, but if this is true, then it certainly is good news, isn't it? What do you think they'll do now? Interview the mother?'

The question was a reminder that Colin was still relatively inexperienced. He'd obviously not been involved in a sexual abuse case yet. This would probably be a useful learning experience for him.

'I assume so – if she's in an appropriate mental condition to make a statement, anyway. And they'll hopefully do it quickly,' I added. 'In my experience they don't tend to let the grass grow once they suspect a criminal act has taken place – they can't. Too much risk that the perpetrator's still at it. And perhaps they'll also interview Mrs Gallagher, since she knew the family so well. And since she's claimed to have seen men going in and out of the house, there's a fair chance she'd be able to identify him as well.'

'Well, here's hoping,' Colin began, then his gaze moved behind me. 'Uh-oh,' he said. 'I think we have trouble.'

I turned around to see an angry-looking young woman approaching, with a little girl perched on her hip. The child looked around four, perhaps a little younger, and was crying, very loudly and lustily. Though because of injury or indignation, I couldn't tell.

The woman stabbed a finger back towards the play area, where Colin, taking the initiative, was now headed. 'Is the boy in the yellow top your son?' she asked me, clearly upset. 'Because he needs sorting out if he is!'

'I'm his foster carer,' I told her.

The change in her expression was marked and immediate. 'Well, *that* figures,' she said. 'I might have known.'

'What's happened? What's he done?'

153

She twisted around so I could take a look at her little girl's arm. 'He's bitten my daughter is what he's done. See the teeth marks? Absolute disgrace. You've no business letting animals like that out in public. I've half a mind to call the police, the little sod!'

So, the child's tears had been of pain, then. About which I felt genuinely sorry. Sam had clearly bitten her pretty hard because I could still see the tiny teeth marks. But another feeling muscled in that was slightly less noble – an instinctive anger that, now she knew Sam was in care, this woman was talking in such derogatory tones. Kids had spats all the time and though I'd never condone it, and would of course reprimand Sam the very minute Colin brought him back, her automatic use of the term 'animal' in Sam's case upset me almost as much as what he'd done.

It was a feeling I knew I must temper, and I tried to, but just as I was launching into 'I'm so sorry, I'll speak to him,' she immediately spoke over me, with a follow-up of 'Speak to him? *Speak* to him? At the very least he deserves a hiding. As if talking will ever sort out a kid who behaves like that! Bloody goodie-goodie claptrap. You just keep him away from my daughter.'

I was shaken by her vehemence, but I'm not generally given to biting my tongue – and in this case the urge to point out the flaw in her childcare philosophy was strong. To tell her that suggesting violence was hardly the best way I could think of as a way to *stop* a child being violent. That wasn't being a goodie-goodie – it was just plain old common sense.

I held my tongue though, and as she turned around and marched away, I turned my attention, as I'd promised, to a returning, and now red-in-the-face Sam.

'How could you hurt that girl, love?' I asked him, as Colin sat down again. 'You must know that you shouldn't hurt someone like that – especially a little person like she was.'

Sam remained defiant. 'She was sat on top of the slide and wouldn't move for me,' he said. 'I tried asking nicely, but she *still* wouldn't move. Then she called me a bad name.'

I'll bet, I thought. *Perhaps 'sod'?* Like mother, like daughter? Though Sam's eyes were downcast as he spoke, so at least it seemed he knew he was in the wrong.

'So then you should have left her there and come to find me or Colin,' I went on. 'And *we* would have sorted it out for you. You can't just go around hurting people to get your own way, love.'

Sam met my gaze then, and held it. He seemed genuinely puzzled now. 'That's what grown-ups do, don't they? Why are they allowed and I'm not?'

I was too stunned by his logic to answer that question. Not immediately, at any rate. Because, to him, it was pertinent. He had experienced for himself – as we'd seen only an hour previously – that if a grown-up wanted something, they simply went right on and took it, regardless of him getting hurt.

Thankfully, Colin stepped in to rescue me.

'I know it sometimes seems that way, buddy, and you're right to ask the question. But that doesn't mean they're in the right. They are in the *wrong* – it's never okay to hurt someone else like that. Doesn't matter if they're a kid *or* a grown-up.'

Sam pouted. 'They still do though.'

'You're right, Sam. Sometimes they do. But that doesn't mean they *should* do. And you shouldn't either.'

'Superheroes do.'

'Ah, but that's just it. They don't. They might fight the baddies, but that's a different thing entirely. And something you might want to think about. They fight the baddies to stop *them* from hurting innocent people. Not to get their own way. That's not what they're about. They're about doing good for others. Being brave, and being *helpful*. And, ah,' – he glanced up – 'about refuelling by eating burgers that are the size of your *face*. Let's eat, shall we?' He grinned across at me as Sam nodded, happier now. 'After all, who ever saved the world on an empty stomach?'

I smiled back, thinking Colin might have missed his vocation – as a politician, perhaps, or after-dinner speaker. But I immediately realised the silliness of the thought. He hadn't missed his vocation – far from it. He'd found it.

And I had another thought. That the cliché was right. That not all superheroes wore capes.

Chapter 15

While I had put a lot of thought into planning how to prepare Sam for his police interview, I hadn't spent the same amount of time wondering how he'd respond to it, because you just can't predict these things with any accuracy. Anyway, wasn't 'expect the unexpected' my personal mantra?

But if I'd expected anything it would have been a return of Sam's nightmares, because revisiting what had happened to him would surely stir everything up again. And nightmare he did have, that very night. Where I *was* slightly surprised (and I fully admit this was ridiculous) was that, even given that there was still so much to learn about Sam, he responded to his nightmare in such an unlikely, visceral way.

When we returned home after the meeting, he was still full of beans; having put the skirmish with the little girl behind him, he was in good spirits, both about the ball pool and spending time with Colin.

He played with the Lego for some considerable time, both before and after tea, building various complex traps for catching bad guys. Which struck me as worth noting, because it was a positive way to go about addressing the re-imagining of his personal horrors. I duly did so. We also went out into the garden to gather a collection of little pebbles, so he could add to his stock of important counting things. I figured, with what we'd stirred up in him today, he might need them.

I also had a brainwave. 'How about beans as well?' I suggested. 'Did you know that people who count money for a living are sometimes known as bean counters?'

'Are there money beans?' he asked.

'No, but have you ever heard the expression "I haven't got a bean"? That's what people sometimes say when they have no money. I think it came from *Jack and the Beanstalk* – when Jack sold the cow for a handful of magic beans. Do you know that story?'

'I don't know, I don't think so.'

'It's a very famous fairy tale. Jack climbs the beanstalk he grows from the magic beans he sold his mother's cow for, and at the top he finds a giant. And all sorts besides. Tell you what,' I said, as I pulled out a bag of dried haricot beans from the back of the cupboard for him, 'you count out a hundred of those while I go and find my big book of fairy tales. Then I can read it to you, can't I? You'll like Jack. He's a bit of a superhero himself, just like you.'

And by the time Sam had had a bath and gone to bed, and I'd read him *Jack and the Beanstalk*, I even allowed myself a small pat on the back. He was processing his traumas, we'd made measurable progress, we would continue to make progress, I was sure of it.

But that pride of mine was clearly setting itself up for a major fall. And from a greater height than previously, because when I woke refreshed the following morning after an unbroken night, I blithely assumed Sam had slept through as well.

That he had not was apparent as soon as I went in to wake him, however – at around nine, long after Mike and Tyler had left for work and college, and purposely late because if he was exhausted by the previous day's dramas then it made sense to let him sleep on till he woke naturally.

But he'd been awake a good while, I judged, and given the state of his bedroom had spent a good part of the night awake as well. He was still in pyjamas, but not the ones he'd gone to bed in. At some point, he'd fetched his favourite pair from the washing basket in the bathroom and, given the state of his bedding, had done some serious thrashing about. Three of the four drawers in his chest were gaping open, contents spewing, and spaces in the same made it clear without my even looking that he'd had all his collections of counting things out.

And there was something about his expression that made me stop myself giving him the now usual hair ruffle and kiss on the head. 'Morning, sleepy head!' I said instead, sticking with my usual jaunty morning tone. 'I've been waiting for you to get up so we can have breakfast together.' No response. Nor would he meet my eye. I sat down on the edge of his bed. 'Sam? Are you okay, sweetie?'

'Get out,' he said. And said it evenly, but with an undertone of contained anger.

So I was persona non grata. Because of the reprimand about the girl yesterday? Or because he'd begun to think more about the disclosures he'd shared yesterday, and what the implications might be?

I dismissed my first thought – the latter – because would Sam do that? Really? Sam didn't think about consequences. Definitely not negative consequences. Yes, he understood the relationship between chores and getting stars, but that, up to now, had been as far as it went.

'Okay,' I said, equally evenly. 'I can do that, if you want me to. But I can see something is bothering you, love. Can we talk about it?'

Sam's reaction was instantaneous. He'd been sitting on his bed but now he sprang up into a crouch, then, using his legs as pistons, he pounced at me. And when I say 'pounced', I mean 'pounced', just like an animal. Which took me by surprise, because it had been weeks since he'd been violent towards me. But, boy, was he making up for that now. He had both hands buried in my hair, each gripping a clump, which made my scalp scream, and was using his legs now to knee me in the thighs and stomach.

'Get out, get out!' he screamed. 'I don't want you no more! You maked me tell!'

I shouted back, equally loudly, using the force of my voice in the hope of shocking him into submission. 'Sam!'

I barked. 'Stop this right now!' I grabbed both his wrists as I spoke, but that did nothing to loosen his grip on my hair, so while my thighs continued to take a battering, I let go with one hand and used it to untangle one set of his fingers. I then held on tightly to his released hand and tried one-handed to release the other – which, given the strength of his grip, was no mean feat.

Having finally managed it, I then held onto both his hands, very firmly, and slowly brought them down to his sides. And as I bent my head down to try for eye contact, I had a stupid thought – that I must look like Medusa, and maybe that would scare him into calming down. 'Can you hear me, Sam?' I said – again loudly enough to be heard over his yelling, 'I said stop this right now, and settle down so you can tell me what is upsetting you.'

'*You* are! You and stupid Sampson and that Kim woman. You're all crazy if you think that bad guy isn't coming for you now. For me too! He's gonna kill us all now!'

'That's silly, Sam,' I said. 'No one knows you're here. No one can get you at this house. You are safe. This is a safe house,' I added, warming to my theme. 'You were brought here in secret. Just like superheroes do with people *they're* protecting. And when Kim finds out who the bad man is, she'll see to it that he can't hurt anyone ever again. Do you understand that, Sam? Do you hear me?'

Sam met my eyes then. And stopped thrashing about as suddenly as he'd started. Then he leapt from the bed, and bolted from the room. 'Don't care!' he screamed as he thundered down the stairs. I followed, just in time to see him heading into the kitchen where, as I entered, he was ripping the chart from its new permanent home on the back of the conservatory door.

'Sam! *Stop* that!' I called out. 'Calm down and *think* before destroying your chart. Think about all those points you've earned – you realise that you won't be able to earn all your stars today if you continue to behave like this?'

'Don't care about the stupid stars,' he yelled back, 'or pizza or burgers or movies! Don't care about *none* of that stuff.' He then screwed up the chart and threw it down on the floor, jumping up and down and stamping on it as he raged.

I knew that to intervene at this point wouldn't be wise, so, instead, without saying anything further, I walked across to the dining area and sat down at the table. There was a now cold, half-mug of coffee on it so I picked it up and started to sip it. I wanted Sam to see that I was calm and not reacting. And, eventually, it seemed to work. After a good minute's stand-off – Sam glaring at me with clenched, white-knuckled fists, while I pretended to leaf through a pile of Mike's left-out managerial paperwork, while stealing sideways, corner-of-the-eye glances – his shoulders finally dropped. He then kicked the chart across the floor and marched past me into the living room. The TV came on moments later. At which my own shoulders dropped a little – I had been prepared for crashes and bangs. And when I looked in on him, he was sprawled on the sofa.

I slipped back into the kitchen, thinking that, after a period of time, Sam would do as he usually did and start to behave better, deploying his well-honed skill at seemingly forgetting his rages. In the interim, it was just a waiting game so I made myself another coffee and took it, and my mobile, out into the back garden, where another bright spring day had got under way, oblivious to the squalls and storms within.

Once I was sitting down, I took the opportunity to call Christine Bolton. She needed an update on the events of the interview yesterday anyway and though I'd obviously log and send an account of this morning, I still favoured the old-fashioned business of chatting stuff through on the phone.

'Bless him,' she said once I'd given her an account of how betrayed Sam now felt about us 'making' him talk. 'It's a great shame this has created difficulties with the points programme, too, because it seemed to be working so well. But hopefully it's only going to be temporary collateral. Once he realises his fears aren't going to become reality, I'm sure he'll begin to trust that we all have his best interests at heart. Listen, would you like me to see if I can get someone to come out and help reassure him on that score?'

'No, that's fine,' I said. 'I'm sure this is only temporary, as you say. I just wanted to put you in the picture, touch base. Here's hoping there's progress once his mother has been interviewed, and we're in a position to back up our reassurances with hard facts. Though it makes no difference to Sam now, it would be good to know the law's on to him, wouldn't it?'

'Absolutely. And the very minute I hear anything on that score, I'll let you know. Or Colin will, obviously. In the meantime, since you're on, any chance we could get a date in our respective diaries for your next supervision visit? I've been checking my lists and I think yours is overdue.'

Supervision is a vital component in fostering, and an ongoing one. Every six weeks, a supervising social worker (who, in our case, was also our link worker, Christine) is required to make an official visit to the foster carers on their list, to check on the standard of fostering they provide. Naturally, it also involves a lengthy, official form, which covers areas such as a child's diet, their medical appointments, their daily routine and so on, plus a person-alised checklist to ensure the carers are following the initially agreed individual care plan. The foster carer is expected to give clear examples of how they have met the government standards of care, and details about how they've addressed any given 'flashpoint', or difficult situ-ation, and then provide feedback about how they think they could improve, if they felt they could have handled things in a different way. Pretty standard stuff, really, but all of it important. And to a new carer, it could be both intimidating and daunting. It was something I remem-bered very well.

These days, however, I approached these sessions differently. Not as opportunities for the powers-that-be to find us wanting, but more as brainstorming sessions where I could pause and reflect, and add to my stock of strategies and skills. There was something new to learn with every child, after all. And much to be gained from the confidence-building business of it being confirmed that, in the moment, you chose the right strategy.

As I'd clearly done this morning, with Sam. When I came back indoors, having arranged a date for Christine's visit, it was to find the chart back in place, slightly crumpled, but still functional, and Sam back where I'd left him, watching TV on the sofa.

'Is it breakfast time yet?' he asked, when he'd realised I'd come in. 'I'm as starving as the biggest giant in giantland!'

I pushed my sleeves up and unthinkingly ran my hands through my knotted hair. *Ouch!* And as strong as one too, I thought wryly.

Chapter 16

Sam's 'silent protest', as in the nightmare during which he'd elected not to seek my reassurance, was, it turned out, a temporary measure. Because the next night he seemed to suffer terrors for its duration, and I wore a path through the landing carpet trying to calm him.

I first woke to hear him screaming, having woken from a horrible nightmare, the details of which, though, he still refused to share with me. But though I knew he was worried I'd 'tell' to 'the others', he at least let me cuddle him and coax him back to sleep. I'd then woken, just under an hour later, to hear him howling. On that occasion he was sitting bolt upright in bed, head thrown back, like a little wolf-boy.

Again I calmed him and, once I had, I also reminded him that howling so loud woke the whole house up, at which, touchingly and heartbreakingly, he apologised for being 'such a nuisance' and tearfully promised that he wouldn't howl again.

And he didn't. My third awakening was to the sound of what appeared to be something heavy being dragged across a room. And when I went to check, it was to find that my ears hadn't deceived me; it took some considerable time to get the door open. I pushed my way in to reveal that both sets of bedside drawers had been relocated in a bid to block the door. 'I dreamed the bad man was trying to get me,' Sam told me, sobbing. 'Can you stay with me till I go to sleep?'

So I had, and by the time Mike had gone off to work, and Tyler to college, I would have loved to burrow under my own duvet for a couple of hours. I couldn't, though, because I'd already made plans. I'd arranged for Kieron to call up with Luna, after dropping Dee Dee at school, so he could take Sam and both dogs out for an hour. It seemed the most likely way to distract him from his demons and would also give me time to sit and gather my thoughts about the best way to move forward with the placement, both in terms of Sam's emotional well-being and as a statement of intent – one that I could present to Christine, to hopefully inspire a bit more action in terms of assessment and schooling. The school Easter holidays were almost upon us, after all, and if he wasn't back in education of some sort for the summer term, we'd be looking at September. And, though the disclosures about a possible abuser were no less important, Sam's education was, arguably, more so.

But to say I was pleased to get a call from Colin Sampson was an understatement.

'You should be getting an email yourself, I think,' Colin said, 'but I got one this morning from Kim Dearing, regarding her interview with Sam's mother. And from what I'm reading, there's clearly no love lost between her and Mrs Gallagher. Which I think we already knew, didn't we? But it seems Mrs Gough has her own thoughts on Mrs Gallagher. She says – let me read it – "she's a busy-body, a bloody liar and a troublemaker".'

'As she would, I suppose,' I said. 'She's obviously going to fight her corner. But it's still a bit rich given that Mrs Gallagher appears to have been the only glue holding that family together over the years. Look how often she stepped in to pick up the pieces whenever there was a crisis.'

'My thoughts too,' Colin said. 'But she's apparently made it quite clear to the police that she wishes she never accepted any help from the woman in the first place. Said that all their neighbour ever did was made her feel inferior and then gossiped about her to anyone who'd listen.'

'Well, there's probably something in that bit,' I said. 'Look how quick Mrs Gallagher was to spill the beans about her to us. Doesn't mean she's a bad woman, of course. Better to be a gossip and actually care about the children's welfare than be a gossip and not get involved.'

'I agree,' Colin said. 'But Mrs Gough apparently swears blind that there were no boyfriends – at least not for the last few years. She said – and I think she shows emotional intelligence in doing so – that her illness prevented her from forming relationships, that how on earth did they imagine she'd have sustained any?'

'So it's definitely an illness then?' I asked, slightly embarrassed. Like many others, I imagined, I'd leapt too easily to the conclusions that had been planted in my head by Mrs Gallagher. 'As in a recognised condition?'

'Indeed it is,' Colin said. 'She's still undergoing assessment and will be detained under the Mental Health Act – I can't remember which section offhand, but she'll be there for quite some time, it seems. But she's definitely had a psychotic episode, and is currently being medicated, so yes, it's safe to say she does have some form of mental illness.'

'And what else? Did Kim Dearing ask her about the episodes of Sam being locked in the dog cage?'

'Yes, she's admitted that on occasion she did put the boy in a dog kennel. But again she is adamant that it isn't what it seems. She admits that she did put him in there a couple of times as a punishment – when she was at her wits' end because of his behaviour towards his siblings. But she stresses that she never actually locked him in there. Not for more than ten minutes or so.'

'Even so,' I said. 'So the kid gets on your nerves, and it's okay to just throw him in a cage?'

'I know, but her point is that after those isolated incidents, it was always Sam who put *himself* in the dog cage.'

A memory returned. Of Sam asking if he could have a dog cage. So it wasn't just a version of Stockholm syndrome, then, where captive people grow to trust and identify with their captors. If what Mrs Gough said was true, it genuinely was Sam's safe place.

'D'you remember that?' I said to Colin, once I'd mused on it out loud.

'I do indeed,' he said. 'You live and learn, eh? Anyway, the other news to come out of this is that solicitors and guardians are being appointed for all the siblings now, so we can go to court to get a full care order for each of them. There's no chance any of them will be going back home. Not that the mother wants them back anyway.'

'She's made that clear?'

'Yes, she's made that clear.'

Another reality that made me wish I believed in unicorns. No, of course I wouldn't have wanted the children to be sent back to such an uncaring mother, but to know that she didn't want them anyway was just an extra bit of damage to add to their already blighted lives. They were all young now, so there was hope, but I also knew from experience that when children in care became teenagers, they wanted to know the ins and outs of it all, no matter how hard it was to hear. And I also knew that the effect of hearing truths like this, warts and all, often had life-changing and devastating results.

'Okay,' I said sighing, 'I don't think I expected any different, if I'm honest. But the thing is, where do we go from here? Sam says he was abused, and I believe him, Mrs Gallagher has hinted that lots of men were regular visitors to the house, and now the mother says that's all codswallop. Surely that can't be the end of it?'

'No, not at all,' Colin said. 'At the end of Kim's email she assures me that they will continue to make enquiries and that, at some point, Sam will have to be interviewed again, I'm afraid. Still an informal setting, but he will be pressed to disclose some more.'

As if things weren't bad enough. Sam already had me down as the tell-tale who started this ball rolling in the first place, and if I didn't do some serious damage control, it would definitely have an impact on our future relationship.

And, by extension, his future.

'Wish me luck, then,' I said, after telling Colin about the previous night, and my fears that it would get worse after another interview. 'I'm not going to tell him yet, though. I need to find a way to let him see I'm not the enemy before we go down that particular road again.'

'You'll be fine, Casey,' Colin said. 'I don't know Sam as well as you yet, but I do know that he holds you in high regard – you and Mike – so although he might be a bit confused right now about who to blame, I'm sure he'll work it out for himself in time.'

Despite Colin's supportive words, I was feeling pretty low by the time I hung up the phone. I stared up at the ceiling, in the direction of Sam's bedroom, and wished that I had the superhero ability to freeze time. Just for a few hours, I thought, just so that Sam didn't have to wake up feeling frightened and wrung out again. So I had longer to try and think of some way I could start to fix all this.

'But you can't, Mum,' Kieron said after I poured my heart out to him. Sam was still asleep, unsurprisingly, and I was loath to go and wake him. So, since my son was in no rush, we at least had time to chat. Well, for me to gabble on and him to listen. Since when did my son become my counsellor? 'Mum, you can't fix everything,' he pointed out, as Luna pattered round the kitchen. 'And you shouldn't try to. Colin's right. It's going to take time – you, of all people, should know that. You know what your problem is?'

'Enlighten me, dear son,' I said. 'But then I suggest you duck before I have to swipe you one.'

Kieron grinned. 'You always try to be everything to everyone. And that can't always work, Mum. It does for some kids, to have a mummy figure who's also a therapist, a teacher, a psychologist, and so on. But for kids like Sam – well, I reckon he's a bit like I was, don't you? And all he needs is a mum. To go to when he's scared. He won't expect the answers. He won't expect explanations. He just needs a cuddle and the knowledge that you're there.'

I blinked at Kieron. When exactly did my son get to be so bloody grounded?

He caught my expression. 'I'm pretty damned amazing, aren't I?' he said, laughing. 'That'll be ten pounds please. Oh, and that's with the family and friends discount.' He then stood up, reached down for Luna, and tucked her under his arm. 'Now I'm off for my next session, upstairs, with a certain young man, and I'm taking my assistant up with me.' He tipped his head to the side. 'So just leave it on the table.'

Chapter 17

Life is full of contradictions, and, over the next few days, life at home with Sam seemed to have become one. I found myself in the very unusual position of being seen as both the enemy and the saviour. There was no doubt, as he struggled to come to terms with having revealed his secret, that Sam blamed me for making him tell. But at the same time, now that he felt so vulnerable and exposed, I appeared to be the one person who he could hide behind.

And 'hide behind' in a very literal sense. He became extremely clingy, following me around the house as I went from room to room, anxious not to let me out of his sight. The only times in the day when I was parted from my little shadow was when Kieron came round and they would go off to walk Flame and Luna together.

This too was an unusual situation. It was definitely fortuitous that Kieron's work situation (he was working through an accumulation of untaken annual leave) meant he was free most mornings *to* help – what had proved workable for him and Laura as a way to manage Dee Dee's school runs slotted perfectly with my need to call on him to 'babysit' Sam. But it was normally Riley who stepped in to help out with any of our foster children, not least because she was a trained foster carer herself.

But it was definitely Kieron who Sam had struck up a bond with, perhaps because, in some ways, they recognised their similarities. Which was lovely for Sam, and, on the face of it, likewise for Kieron – I certainly never pressured him to help me in any way. But still I worried. Sam was a complex little boy, and however genial their walks and talks, I fretted about the pressure it might place on my son, who had never coped that well with pressure.

But it was what it was, and for the moment it was a godsend. And, for Sam, who was so isolated – entirely without friends and family – the blossoming of such a friendship could only ever be a good thing.

All that said, Sam wasn't stupid.

'You're sending me out a lot, Casey,' he observed, on the morning of Christine's visit, when I told him it was time to get dressed, ready for Kieron's arrival. 'Why aren't you coming too?'

'Because I have a meeting, sweetie,' I said as I handed him his T-shirt. 'And besides, when you and Kieron have both dogs with you, you run too fast for me. I can't keep up with you. Not with my little legs.'

'What meeting?' Sam asked, looking at me as his head poked through the top of his T-shirt. 'Is it going to be about me again?'

'Not this time,' I answered, pleased that this was true. 'Remember Mrs Bolton? Christine? The lady who brought you to us? It's her who is coming over, and today it is all about me.'

'About what?'

'About my job, and how I'm doing it.'

He looked confused. 'What job? You mean like Mike's job? I didn't know you had a job.'

Ah, from the mouths of babes, I thought. Then struggled a little with how to answer. 'My job taking care of you,' I plumped for eventually. 'You know, making sure everything is as it should be. And making charts so you can earn all those sticky stars,' I added. 'Anyway, it's all very boring. So you don't need to be here. And wouldn't you rather be out in the park with Kieron and the dogs?'

Sam nodded and tugged his top down, then leaned down to lace his trainers. 'Course,' he said. 'But I'm coming right back again, aren't I? And you're still going to be here?'

'Course I will be, silly. I'll be waiting right here for you. And I'll have snacks ready for when you're back, okay?'

It seemed it was, because he trotted off with Kieron happily enough. But as I waved them off, I reminded myself I must press Christine about assessment – a boy of Sam's age really needed to be in school, making friends who were his own age. And the longer he wasn't, the harder it would be.

So it was the first thing I asked Christine when she arrived.

'Ah,' she said, her expression pained. 'About that ...'

'That sounds ominous.'

'Not ominous exactly,' she said, sipping her tea. 'More irritating. The truth is that we did get the referral through –'

'*What*?'

'*And* an appointment,' she continued. 'Which I'm afraid we've had to cancel. At least postpone for the moment.'

It took a moment for this to sink in. Except it didn't. Appointments for assessment were like manna from heaven. You didn't cancel them. You clung to them as if your very life depended on them. '*What?*' I said again. 'But –'

'Because of the probable necessity for further police interviews,' she explained. 'The psychologist we spoke to said it would all be too much for Sam – that he'd only end up even more traumatised and confused. It was felt that it would be better to get to the bottom of all this first. That it would be better to hold off working with him till he's had time to process what he's *already* having to deal with. Which is a fair point.'

'Oh, I know. And I *do* understand. But, God – what a mess! These bloody appointments take *so* long to get, and when we finally get one, we have to let it go. Typical. Grrr!'

Christine laughed. 'I knew you wouldn't be amused,' she said. 'But it's the right thing to do. Imagine Sam having to deal with all that, in the middle of all this. He just wouldn't cope, would he?'

I was busy imagining the next three or four months – of Sam languishing at home while the world whizzed on without him. But Christine was right. To throw formal assessment interviews and tests into the current mix would be highly likely to destabilise him even further. And, by extension, shunt that precious school place even further into the far distance. And with no guarantees that the police investigation would even come to anything – anything that could benefit Sam, more specifically – it felt like the worst of all worlds.

But there was no point in wishing things were otherwise. That appointment had flown now, to someone else's benefit. 'No, you're right,' I conceded. 'I suppose we'll just have to hope the police make some progress.'

'Which I'm pushing for, believe me,' Christine said. 'They know the score. Speaking of which' – she was already rummaging in her laptop bag – 'shall we crack on and zip through all the paperwork?'

Which wasn't paperwork. Our organisation had finally wheezed its way into the twenty-first century, and all the supervision paperwork was now on the screen of her newly gifted tablet, complete with the means for me to sign it off once done – not with a pen, but my fingertip.

'But is this even legal?' I asked, once we'd ploughed through all the pages and I drew a cack-handed approximation of my signature with my finger.

'Apparently so,' she reassured me. 'Though I don't feel quite on board yet. To be honest it terrifies me every time I close it down, in case I lose everything I've done. Truth be told, I'd much rather scribble in my notepad. At least I know my work is safe then. Because you never know, do you? I know I sound like a dinosaur, but it genuinely appals me that so much confidential stuff is virtual these days.' She closed the cover on the tablet and patted it with her hand. 'Can you imagine the repercussions if some of what we store here got hacked?'

'Tell me about it,' I said. And said with feeling. 'Technology is fast becoming the bane of my fostering life.'

Which led to a happy interlude, where, free from the censure of any sniggering young people, we banged on about our mutual mistrust of the modern world, the way everything was moving too fast to keep up with and how apparently straightforward stuff, like updating the software on our smartphones, sometimes felt like a terrifying leap of faith.

'Honestly, you should have seen me with my mother-in-law at the weekend,' Christine told me. 'We've got her on the internet – finally! – so she can manage all the household finances, and setting it all up has been the epitome of the blind leading the blind. You need a whole new dictionary just to navigate the flipping acronyms! Do *you* know what an IP address is? I'm still not sure I do. It'll be a miracle if she manages a week before we go into total meltdown and she pays her gas money to the phone people and vice versa.'

'How are things going generally?' I asked her. Her father-in-law had dementia – one of the reasons she'd moved to our area in the first place – and, having deteri-orated very quickly, was now facing a move into a home specialising in end-of-life care. I felt for her mother-in-law. I also felt for her. It was a grim road that many of us would be travelling eventually, and I knew managing it must take a lot of her emotional energy. Not to mention actual energy.

'Oh, okay,' she said. 'We tend to take a "day-by-day" approach. Still firefighting, obviously. Till we get him where he's safe. When we're going to reward ourselves with a few days away. Feels like an age since we'd had a day when we've dared switch our phones off. But the light is there, at the end of the tunnel at least –' She smiled ruefully. 'Well, if we squint a bit. Speaking of which, I have good news on the respite front finally. Well, more an idea to run by you.'

We were in the kitchen, and I was by now making more tea and coffee. 'That sounds intriguing,' I said, as I returned with our mugs.

'Unconventional,' she said, 'but it might just be perfect. I was struggling to get someone for your dates – 'twas ever thus, eh? – and I happened to be chatting to Sam's siblings' social worker, Linda, and she came up with what I think is the perfect resolution.'

'Go on, then. Spill,' I said. I could tell she was enjoying keeping me in suspense.

'Well, we thought we might ask Maureen Gallagher. It just so happens that she's already done respite for the other Gough children.'

'Really?' This *was* intriguing. 'So she fosters, does she?'

'Not officially. It came up during a similar situation to yours. It was one of the children who suggested it, apparently. They'd been talking a lot about her, and asking if and when they could see her – she was clearly a big presence in their lives. And when they checked it out – well, checked her out, CRB check and so on – it seemed eminently workable. Seems she's been a bit of a lifeline down the years. When Mum had to go into hospital, or was having a crisis, and so on – one of those unsung carers you always hear about, and probably one of the main reasons they've not come into the system before.'

'And she'd be happy to have Sam too?'

'Well, we've not run it by her yet, but I see no reason why not. Assuming she's free, of course. I thought I'd ask you first. I mean, equally, we could look further afield for a respite carer for a couple of days, but I just thought it might be less traumatic for Sam to be with someone he already knows and cares about.'

'Absolutely,' I said. 'Particularly the way he is currently. And when Colin and I went to see her she spoke about him with what seemed genuine tenderness.' I did a mental date check. 'I'm surprised she never said anything to us when we were there.'

'Probably didn't think it her place to. Confidentiality and all that. Anyway, I'll get on and ask her. And if it's a goer I was thinking that maybe you and Mike might like to pop round and see her? Just thinking ahead really – as you do! – about the ongoing situation. Because you never know, she might just turn out to play an ongoing role in the kids' lives.'

'God, you're worse than me!' I said.

'I've learned from the master. But why not? If there's anything positive we can haul from the wreckage of those kiddies' childhoods, I'm all for grabbing it with both hands. Aren't you?'

I agreed that I was. And another thought occurred to me. Delicate, under the circumstances, because Christine had lost a daughter to cot death, very young. But perhaps she would know. 'Speaking of childhoods, do you know anything about what happened to her son Sean? There were so many pictures of him around the place, and a couple of the things she said ... but I didn't want to be nosy. Did he die young, do you know?'

'No, he didn't die,' Christine said. 'He's very much alive. But not well. Not well at all, bless him. All very tragic. He was born with congenital brain injuries, and will never be able to live a normal, independent life. He's in his thirties now, apparently. Lives in a residential home.'

'Wow,' I said, trying to take it all in, and finding it all falling into place. 'No wonder she feels the way she does about Sam's mother. The way those little ones have been treated. The abuse Sam has suffered. She'd probably have given anything just to have a healthy child, wouldn't she? No wonder she feels so protective towards those children. And, God, it all makes sense now – what she said when we were there. Not sure if I mentioned it in my notes, but I remember it because it seemed such an odd thing to comment. She said that *whatever* you were given, you had to do your very best for them. Now I know why. God, it's all so sad, isn't it?'

Which it was, and I brooded on it for the rest of the morning. While Mike was more pragmatic (when I texted him, he replied with 'Hurrah! Mini-break back on the agenda down the line then???'), I couldn't stop thinking about life being such a lottery. About Mrs Gallagher, and the sense of loss that must weep from her very pores.

So it was a wake-up call – to be sure to keep counting our own blessings. To remember that, if you looked, you could find sad stories everywhere.

But what I didn't know, because I couldn't know, was that it wasn't just sad. It would turn out to be oh so much more.

Chapter 18

It wasn't usual practice for a social worker to work with the children on their books at the weekends. Not that social work was ever just a nine-to-five job, because there were always occasions when the unexpected happened. But unless a social worker was on call, weekends were free time – well, in theory. They, like us, were always dogged by endless paperwork. It was also Easter weekend, and though we weren't planning to make any sort of fuss (this year, Riley was going to be away with her in-laws, so it wouldn't be much more than a quick Easter egg hunt for Dee Dee, at Kieron's), others did, I knew. So I was extremely grateful when Colin Sampson agreed to help us out with Sam the following Saturday, so that Mike and me could go to Mrs Gallagher's and talk about the potential upcoming respite.

We decided not to tell Sam where we were going, though. Just that Colin was coming over with an Easter egg, and wanted to spend time with him. It made sense –

if either we or Mrs Gallagher changed our minds about Sam staying over with her, ignorance would be bliss; we wouldn't find ourselves in the position of having built up Sam's hopes only to dash them again.

Not that we needed to. Sam was as oblivious to the business of Colin having weekends off from work as he was to the notion that what I did was 'work'. He was on a high about Colin coming and the 'big Easter adventure' they were going on, and if it even crossed his mind that there was a reason for us going off for a few hours he was too busy thinking about his own day to ask me.

'We're going on a very long journey,' he told me as he paced the carpet by the front window. He was speaking to me, but as much to himself. He looked deep in thought, head down, hands linked together behind his back – a bit like a little old man ruminating on life. 'It's a *very* long journey,' he added. 'And I think that's a clue. I think it's a puzzle Sampson wants me to solve.'

'I just think Colin means you'll be out and about for a while, love,' I suggested, anxious that Sam might have got the wrong end of the stick and was setting himself up for disappointment. I'd heard them talking on the phone – they fell so easily into deep conversation – and though it was clear Colin had a knack of understanding Sam's level, it also meant that I frequently lost track of what either of them were on about. Perhaps this was simply one of those occasions and Colin had indeed made plans I didn't know about. 'Anyway, he'll be here soon, so I'm sure all will be clear. In the meantime, if you don't stop all that pacing up and down, you are going to end up wearing out my carpet.'

'Too late,' Mike chipped in from his favourite chair, where he was reading. 'He's flattened all the pile. Uh-oh. We're going to need a new carpet.'

Sam stopped and looked down, then he frowned. 'Oh,' he said. 'I'm sorry. But it's okay, Mike. Don't worry. Me and Sampson will go to the shops and buy a new one.'

I rolled my eyes. Sam took everything so literally, and Mike knew it. 'Stop teasing, you!' I said, flicking him with a tea towel as I walked past. 'Oh, and you can stop pacing now, Sam – looks like your superhero has arrived.'

'Yes!' he said, punching the air and hurrying out into the hall. 'We are going to have the best, *best* day ever!'

'Sure you will, kiddo,' said Mike. 'And make sure you leave some chocolate for me.' He winked at him. 'In lieu of payment.'

A light rain had begun falling by the time we arrived at Mrs Gallagher's, which lent an even gloomier atmosphere to the tired estate we'd driven through, and, because it was much on my mind anyway, to the life she might have lived here with her profoundly disabled child.

And her husband? She'd said he'd been the 'spit of his dad'. But there'd been no mention of Dad, and no hint as to where he was. Was he dead? Were they divorced? What had happened to him? I remembered the sadness in her voice, so one or the other, presumably. Perhaps we would find out today.

'What's she like, then?' Mike asked, as he eyed the neat front garden. And, while trying to describe her, I realised my instinctive first impressions had already changed to more nuanced second ones. In my mind she was no longer the same outspoken, down-to-earth, strong, no-nonsense, Irish woman – who made no secret of her disdain for and disapproval of her former neighbour – but a tragic figure I had mostly fashioned from my imagination.

So, having softened her, I was a little surprised, ten minutes later, to find her everything she'd first appeared, and more.

Though I made new first impressions as she showed us in – this time to the kitchen – where, once again, there was a pot, ready for tea, and a plate of homemade cakes, including chocolates nests, made out of corn-flakes, in which speckled eggs nestled. Part of a batch made for Sam's brother and sister, perhaps? Possibly. My eyes were then drawn immediately to the fridge-freezer – like a magnet – where an assortment of magnets held a variety of pictures, all executed in crayon, by children's hands.

As Mike sat down, and Mrs Gallagher stood and waited for the kettle, I touched one of the pictures automatically, imagining the little ones whose lives had also been so changed – at least very much from the idealised image I was looking at, of a typical child's house, with smoke coiling from a chimney, clumps of grass below, a big yellow sun overhead and the sky a strip of scribbled blue above it. There was another, too, of a boat. A collection of triangles – a hull and two sails – it was bobbing along atop a deep wavy sea, with six-pointed stars daubed above it.

'I had no idea you'd been looking after Sam's siblings,' I told Mrs Gallagher. 'Not till my link worker told me, anyway. It must be such a comfort for them to be able to spend time with you. Bit of welcome continuity in their lives, I expect.'

Mrs Gallagher nodded. 'And for me,' she said. 'They're a pair of little poppets.' Then, following my eye, 'Oh, sorry. I see what you're saying. Those there, they're not done by the little ones. They're Sean's works of art, those. His masterpieces. My own boy,' she added, glancing across at Mike now. 'He does love doing his pictures. He'd have a crayon in his hand all day long, given half a chance. Can't let him near paint, of course, bless him. He'd probably try to drink it! Away with the fairies, he is, half the time, big lump though he is. He always brings his best with him when he visits.'

I felt my face redden. 'Oh, of course,' I said. 'I'm sorry. I should have thought ...'

She waved a dismissive hand. 'Oh, don't be getting all embarrassed, now. It's an easy mistake to make.'

Mike grinned. 'You'll have to excuse my wife, Mrs Gallagher,' he said. 'Bigger feet than Sasquatch when it comes to putting them in her mouth. Anyway, it goes without saying that we're both extremely grateful that you've agreed to look after Sam for us so we can go to this family wedding. Far better that he's billeted with someone he knows and trusts than being packed off to a stranger's for the night. That's if you're sure you don't mind, of course. It's a lot to ask, I know.'

'Heavens, no,' she said as she filled the enormous teapot. 'What those kiddies need more than anything is a bit of normality. I'd have kicked off to high heaven if they'd not let me – at least now and again. It's all they've known, bless their hearts, and it's the least I can do. I said as much to those policemen who came yesterday.'

'So you've had another visit?' I asked. They were obviously working quicker than I'd dared to hope. Which was all to the good. The sooner they made progress, the sooner they'd talk to Sam again, and, fingers crossed, the sooner the powers that be would be happy to start his assessment.

Mrs Gallagher nodded. 'So who's for tea?' she asked. But the question was clearly rhetorical. After spending some seconds vigorously mashing the leaves in the pot, she proceeded to pour out three cups. Coffee clearly still wasn't on the agenda.

But she did have her own one. 'The cheek of the woman! I told them that too. I call a spade a spade, Mr Watson,' she told Mike. 'So I made sure to put them straight about that hussy calling me a liar. It's her who's the fecking liar – there were *always* men round there. I'm no racist, not in a million years' – she gave me a sideways glance now – 'but the woman had no preference – she had black men, and white men, and every colour in between. No bloody men indeed. Cheek of her!'

I coughed to hide my splutter. 'Indeed,' I said. 'And what did they say? D'you think they took it seriously?'

She looked astonished. 'Of course they did! Because round here it's common knowledge. Ask anyone. Drug dealers and the like beating on her front door at all hours. And I'm not stupid,' she added, narrowing her eyes as she proffered the cakes. 'There's her all cosy in some mental home, having them all on that she's ill. And at the expense of us law-abiding tax payers!'

I caught Mike's expression. I knew he was as surprised at Mrs Gallagher's candour as I had been when I'd first met her. And by her anger, which was a simmering presence in the room. Which was understandable, and my eyes strayed back to the pictures. I felt sorry for her. It was odds-on that she'd struggled all her life with her own son, and had no doubt needed to fight for every little bit of help she could get. No wonder there was so much bitterness in her voice. So thank goodness he was now being taken care of. If he was a child in a man's body – and, from what I'd learned, I imagined he must be – there was no way a lady of Mrs Gallagher's age and stature would be able to look after him on a full-time basis. I knew from experience just how physical a job it could be – had probably been a struggle from the time he'd hit puberty – with, presumably, the usual pubescent dramas. Of course she'd be angry that someone like Sam's mum appeared to get away with whatever she wanted, and though I disagreed with her assessment of her neighbour's 'mental home' as being 'cosy', I certainly understood where she was coming from.

I'd also had a rethink on the empathy front. She might not empathise with Mrs Gough, but with the troubles she'd had, it was evidence of a very kind heart that she cared so much for the little victims of it all. And as she'd been a constant in their short lives, and wanted to continue to be so, I didn't doubt she'd be a positive in Sam's life as well. And if anyone needed positives in his life, little Sam did. Perhaps even more than his brother and sister. Who at least had each other, after all.

We chatted on, about nothing much, Mike admiring her back garden, and, by extension, he got the same tour upstairs as me and Colin had, where, in the drizzle, next door's 'garden' couldn't have provided more of a contrast, the rotting dog enclosure filling more than a third of the space. I wondered, given the situation with Sam's mother, how soon it would become a home again, instead of an eyesore. It couldn't have been nice to live next door to.

Mrs Gallagher pressed us to take a few cakes home. 'Whoever else will eat them?' And though we promised to, because her lemon buns were apparently Sam's favourites, we knew we wouldn't pass them on to Sam himself. So Mike tucked in almost the minute we drove away.

'So, Cinderella,' he said, through a mouthful of cake crumbs, 'looks like you will be going to the ball after all – and without the worry of having to be home by midnight either. And you never know, if it all goes well then the mini-break world is our oyster!'

'Stop being silly,' I said, tutting, and brushing crumbs from the centre console. 'We can't take advantage of the poor woman. And we don't know how it's going to go, so we shouldn't get our hopes up. This is Sam, and he might just hate the idea of going back there, however fond he is of her. And Mrs Gallagher, for all her kindness, might find it all too much. Let's just think one day at a time, at least for now.'

'Oh, my dear wife,' Mike said, 'for all the many sayings your lovely mother taught you, she really didn't teach you the best ones, did she? I mean, what about never looking a gift horse in the mouth?'

I couldn't help but smile. 'Okay, fair enough. But what about not counting your chickens before they're hatched?'

'Okay, touché!' he said. 'But, Case, you have to admit it – I think we've found ourselves a real gem in that woman, don't you?'

I could only agree, even as I didn't want to count chickens. As blunt as she was, Maureen Gallagher was a diamond in the rough, and I was thankful she was now in our lives. A good day, I thought. A productive one, too. Because when we returned it was also to hear all about Sam's 'brilliant' adventure, which had included dog walking, exploring, the bestest burger ever, an egg hunt – he had the loot to show for it too – and being taken to a place that was so special and secret, only the best superheroes knew where it was. Or, in Colin's terms, 'some old country park ruin'.

And that was another plus – that there was such a good connection, right there. Sam might have been the expert in demolishing Lego but the little building blocks were being put in place that would give him some foundations. Stronger ones, hopefully, than those he'd had before.

There was much building to do yet, and perhaps the early blueprints hadn't been perfect, but, brick by brick, we were at least heading upwards. And though I'm not that superstitious, when I went to bed that night, I touched the bedside table before I drifted off to sleep.

So far so good. And – touch wood – that would continue.

Chapter 19

We'd agreed to hold off till the Thursday before the wedding to tell Sam that he was to have a night away from us. I had little choice anyway, because I'd had a last-minute wardrobe panic and, after a slightly frantic bout of intense internet shopping, I had ordered three dresses that were due to arrive that day. So it was that, when the delivery man arrived on the doorstep, I deemed it the right time to put Sam in the picture.

'What's in there?' he wanted to know, once I'd signed for my delivery.

'Ah,' I said. 'Well, they're dresses. Because I'm going to a wedding. I've got to try them on so I can choose one.'

'A wedding? What wedding?' he asked as he followed me upstairs to my bedroom.

'My niece's wedding,' I explained. 'Which is something we need to talk about. It's this coming Saturday, and because it's a long way away, we've arranged for you to go on a special sleepover.'

'A sleepover?' he asked. 'Where? Am I not coming with you?'

'No, love,' I said, as I lay the parcel on my bed. 'Like I said, it's a long way away – a very long way away. So it's not really fair on you to take you along. It's –'

'Why is it not fair?' He looked crestfallen. 'Haven't I been a good boy?'

'Sweetheart, it's not about you being a good boy. Which you have been, no question. But it's not really something I think you'd enjoy. All those people, all strangers. And in a place you don't know –'

'I don't mind. I like strangers.'

This wasn't going well. 'I know, Sam, I know, but we've decided to arrange for you to have your *own* adventure. They're very boring things, weddings, and I'm sure you'd be fed up. So we've arranged an adventure for you. Guess where?'

I'd chosen the right word ('adventure' being one of his favourites) because now, finally, he at least seemed intrigued. 'Is it Kieron's? With Luna?'

I shook my head. 'No, not Kieron's. Kieron will be at the wedding with us. It's –'

'But why can't I just come with you? I'll be a good boy, I promise. Oh –' Something had obviously occurred to him, because he smiled now. 'Is it Sampson's? Am I going on an adventure with Sampson again?'

I slit the seal on the package and the dresses slithered out. I mentally crossed fingers that one of them would fit. There was precious time now to get anything else. But trying them on would have to wait. This was a far more pressing problem.

'No, love, not with Sampson,' I said, going over to the wardrobe for hangers. 'He's not allowed to have you over. He's not allowed to have any kids sleep over,' I added, 'because of his very important job. Have another guess. Have a think. Where else would *you* like to stay over? Who haven't you seen for a long time?'

He was puzzled now, and I could tell he was desperately trying to think. 'I can't guess,' he said eventually, frowning from the effort. 'Well, there's Will and Courtney, but they're not allowed to see me anymore, are they? And I don't *know* anyone else, do I? Who *is* it?'

I wondered who had told him that. Kelly, perhaps? Possibly. Or perhaps someone had said something in the drama of the removal, and he had simply put two and two together and worked it out for himself. I hung the dresses one by one on the back of the wardrobe door, reflecting sadly that, in all probability, he didn't know anyone else, either. Not in any meaningful sense. One truism about children who came into the care system was that they weren't usually brimming with caring friends and relatives, after all. 'Ah, but you do,' I said, trying to keep the mood light. 'How about, let me see ... Mrs Gallagher, your next-door neighbour?'

'Auntie Maureen?' he said, and more confusion crossed his features. 'You mean I'm going to *her* house?'

He immediately shook his head.

Now it was *me* with the confused expression. 'I thought you'd be pleased,' I said. 'Your auntie Maureen certainly is. In fact, she's really excited to be looking after you. She can't *wait* to see you. Sam, why the long face? What's wrong?'

He met my enquiring gaze with an expression I couldn't quite read. Then lowered his own gaze. 'I can't go back to that place.'

I made a mental gear change. I'd obviously touched a nerve with him now. Because this was definitely not the response I'd expected.

I sat down on the bed and patted the space beside me. He climbed on to join me. 'Sweetheart,' I said, 'no one's going to make you go back *there*. Not back to your old *home*. We wouldn't dream of it. You'll be going to Mrs Gallagher's – your auntie Maureen's. She's looking forward to seeing you. I thought you'd be pleased,' I said again. 'Aren't you looking forward to seeing her again?'

Now he nodded. Picked at the duvet cover. 'I s'pose.'

'So what's wrong?'

'I just can't go *back there*.' There were tears in his eyes now. And had it been physically possible, I could have kicked myself. As it was, I could only berate myself, soundly. Of course he was stressed about going back to his old life. To all the sights, sounds and feelings – to igniting memories he was so keen to forget. Because he wasn't like his siblings, was he? He had all his other challenges. And it really hit me now that, in all the weeks we had cared for him, he'd said almost nothing before this – not to us, not to Colin – either about his siblings *or* his mother. All we knew for sure was that a 'bad man' had scared him and hurt him. That he had, briefly, had a puppy. That he had developed a deep need for his 'dog cage'. Of his human family, on the other hand, he had told us precisely nothing. They had been the elephant in the room that we'd always stepped around. When the time came, and he was assessed by CAMHS, and (hopefully) allocated a counsellor, they would no doubt make gentle steps to confront that particular element. But for the time being, if Sam didn't want to talk about his old life then it was central to my job that I not try and make him. To take my lead *from* him, rather than lead him into choppy emotional waters.

And, here, for only the second time, he seemed to be dipping a toe in.

'Can you tell me why, Sam?'

In answer, he didn't speak at first, but snuggled up against my chest. I put my arms around him, feeling his hot little hands against my back. 'Please let me come with you and Mike,' he whispered. 'Please. I'll be good, I'll be *so* good. I don't want to go nowhere. And you *have* to look after me.' His voice began to rise now. 'You can't send me away. It's your job!'

He certainly picked his moment to understand that I had one. 'Sweetheart,' I said, shocked by the urgency of his pleading, 'you're not going back there. You'll be staying with your auntie Maureen, like I said. And she told me you used to go and stay with her all the time. That you used to love it. She said you *really* loved her lemon buns – so she's going to make some for you specially. She's –'

He pulled back. 'But you're not *supposed* to. *You're* supposed to look after me. I'll be a good boy, I promise. I could call you Mummy, if you like, so no one will even *know* I'm not your real kid. *Please* let me come.'

I leaned back too, touched by both the gesture and the logic. 'Sam, love, can you tell me why you don't want to see your auntie Maureen?'

'I *do* want to see her,' he said, crying now. 'But I *told* you. I can't go *back*!'

He scrambled off the bed then, out of the room, and across the landing to his own room. The door slammed. Then silence. I got up and followed him. *What on earth?*

I knocked softly on the door. 'Sam?'

'Go away! I hate you!' came the answer.

My thoughts floundering, I hovered at the door for a few moments in case I heard evidence of things being thrown around. I really didn't know what to make of it all. Was this connected to his autism? No, I doubted it. More likely – most likely – simply a fear of returning. Which was, after all, a perfectly rational response. We had probably been naïve in imagining he'd be okay with it. To be so close to the place where he'd been abused by this nameless 'bad man' would, after all, be an enormous challenge for him.

I headed back downstairs, deep in thought, having a major rethink on what we'd organised. I'd clearly been labouring under a misapprehension. That to spend time with his neighbour – who, admittedly, he didn't seem to have any issue with – would, or at least could, become a positive in his life.

Instead it seemed as if the idea had plunged him off a new emotional cliff. He'd been coping with his traumas by living completely in the moment, and here we were, trying to force him back to the horrors of the past. Perhaps we needed to think again.

But with less than forty-eight hours to go, what were the chances of finding alternative care for him? And even if we did, wouldn't dumping him with a stranger (which is how he'd see it, no question) just make everything one hundred per cent worse? No, it seemed to me that we had only two choices now. Either we took him to the wedding with us, or I stayed at home. Which I'd obviously have to run past Mike once *he* was home.

Though I already knew what his thinking would be. So while Sam stayed in his room – where I was happy to leave him, given that he had a lot to try and process – I went rootling in the spare room for something smart for him to wear.

But if I'd been surprised by Sam's reaction (albeit less so once I'd thought about it) I was even more surprised, when he appeared later that afternoon, by just how much thinking *he* had clearly been doing as well.

Tyler was home by now, and the pair of us were sitting in the kitchen, having a catch-up about the vagaries of our respective days.

'Alright, mate?' Tyler said to Sam as he hovered in the kitchen doorway.

'Cool,' Sam replied, then turned immediately to me. 'Casey,' he asked, 'if I go to auntie Maureen's, how many stars will I earn?'

His look was open and guileless, and because the question was so unexpected, I dithered for a bit before deciding how best to answer. This was such a U-turn and I wasn't sure quite where it had come from. Or, more importantly, where it might be headed. The last thing I wanted was to drag him there against his will, if to do so would set him back emotionally.

'Hmm …' I said, pretending to calculate, but I dithered so long that Tyler clearly felt obliged to answer for me. It was only a matter of seconds but they had obviously seemed to stretch.

'Oh, a lot, I should think,' he said. 'Ten, you reckon, Mum? Twenty? What's the plan, mate?' he added. 'Are you saving stars for something special?'

Sam nodded. 'But it's a secret.' He looked at me once again. 'And Casey,' he added, 'if I go to auntie Maureen's, can it just be for the daytime? So I'm not gone too long? Maybe Sampson could collect me and bring me home again? I'll be a good boy till you're back again, I promise.'

Home again. It made my heart melt. But what was this all about? And was that the answer? To bite the bullet and just drive up and back on the day? I'd yet to speak to Mike, of course, but I'd pretty much decided now that

Sam would simply come with us after all. That I'd ask the B&B we'd booked into if they had a put-you-up bed he could sleep on, next to Tyler.

'Love, we can't leave you home alone. And, you know, I thought you could perhaps come with us after all. I have to speak to Mike, but –'

'No, it's fine,' he said firmly. 'I'll be a good boy and go to auntie Maureen's, and earn lots of stars.'

He really had thought all this through. He was *bargaining* with me.

'Well, as I say, love, I'll have to speak to Mike,' I said. 'Let's see when he gets home, shall we?'

He nodded. Emphatically. Straight-backed, like a little soldier. 'It's fine,' he said again. 'Auntie Maureen will look after me.'

'Of course she will,' I agreed.

'And I'll be good, and she'll play with me. She likes playing with me. She has painting stuff and dinky cars and Lego and *all* sorts.' And with that little pronouncement, he trotted across the kitchen. 'Look, Tyler,' he said, 'have you seen how many stars I've got? And now I'm going to earn even *more*. Are there any difficult jobs for me to do, Casey?'

Sam loved his 'difficult' jobs – particularly sorting the recycling. But I wasn't quite so keen on the difficult job I had myself. To decide whether to take Sam at his word. It was just gone eight, and growing dark, and as I pulled the living-room curtains, I was still trying to fathom what was happening in Sam's head. What had changed. Because something clearly had. Since he'd made his pronouncement, he'd become really chatty about auntie Maureen, describing the games they'd played, the songs they'd sung, the TV programmes they'd watched together, the fairy cakes they'd made and the deliciousness of her lemon buns. Had having time to reflect made him realise he missed her? Had that overridden his fear of re-visiting a place that was so close to his former home?

But then there were the stars, and the secret. I really didn't know what to make of it.

'Well, I don't know what to make of it either,' Mike said, rubbing a hand over his stubble. 'He clearly has a plan on, but what? And why? What's his motivation? Perhaps we should just forget the whole thing and take him with us after all.'

'I wish I could decide what's best,' I said. 'Because he really seems keen to go now. I'm just really anxious now about him being away from us overnight. What if he has one of his night terrors? I think I might call Christine tomorrow. And maybe Colin, too. Get their perspective on it.'

'I doubt they'll have anything to offer that we haven't already considered, love. It's *your* instinct I trust, so whatever you decide is fine by me. And I'm genuinely happy to go up and back in a day if you decide that's best.' He grinned. 'Look on the bright side, it'll spare the kids the embarrassment of my dad-dancing, won't it? And it'll spare you one of your epic Prosecco headaches. And don't look at me like that. Because that's exactly what you will have.'

He was right. I rarely drank, so when I did, I always suffered. And I knew my sister would egg me on, too. 'Or maybe we do just take him.'

'As I say, it's up to you, love. On recent evidence, for what it's worth, I think he'll be fine at the wedding. When was the last time we had a meltdown? As in a major-maelstrom meltdown? And I don't for a minute think Donna will mind if he tags along. Nor Chloe – unless she's come from a completely *different* planet, she'll be on Planet Bride, so, chances are, she'll barely notice he's there.'

By the time I woke up on Friday morning, I was pretty much decided. I'd feel happier if we simply took Sam with us. But would it mean him missing out on a great opportunity? Because I truly felt a continuing relationship with Mrs Gallagher could be good for Sam. I also knew it might help preserve another connection. An even more important one: that with his siblings, something I'd been thinking about a lot.

I knew the official line would remain the same till Sam was formally assessed – that he was so unstable, and violent, that they were better off without him. And possibly he them – after all, he was down as query autistic, and, as night followed day, there would be an automatic assumption that he'd find it hard to form attachments, and that he might end up in residential care anyway.

But once they saw the progress he'd made, they would surely rethink. It might not make a huge difference – it was likely that, at some stage, they would both be adopted; they were both still young enough, anyway – and if that happened the council would have no control over whether a relationship with Sam would continue. But it was surely worth fighting for, wasn't it? And all the time he was in foster care, it would still be on the table. And, in Mrs Gallagher, there was an ongoing link which might otherwise cease to exist.

I said as much to Christine when I called her to update her on developments.

'Exactly,' she said. 'Which is why I think you should stick with Plan A. Yes, it's obviously going to be stressful for him, but perhaps confronting things will help him to open up a bit more. By the way, I was going to email you – there's been a smidge of a development. As in a drug dealer who is already known to the police, who they've established used to supply Mrs Gough with cannabis.'

'So she was definitely doing drugs, then?'

'Seems so. A late admission that has come as a surprise to precisely no one. Which is not to say she doesn't have long-standing mental health issues, because she does. But it does call into question her honesty. Anyway, it's obviously your call, Casey. I can't make the decision for you. But if Sam says he's happy to go to Mrs Gallagher, I'd let him. Linda says she's been a definite force for good for the other little ones, and I'm sure she will be for Sam too.'

No vacillating there, then. So perhaps I was just being over-anxious. And neither was there from Sam. He still wanted to go to Mrs Gallagher, no question.

'I know,' he said, after breakfast, while he was helping me load the dishwasher. 'I should do her a painting. She loves my paintings.'

'That's a great idea,' I said. 'I bet she'd really love that.'

So we got out my art box and he spent half the morning creating a picture for her – of him, Luna and Flame in the park. And as the day unfolded, and his mood remained sunny and cheerful, I began to set aside my concerns about that first, distressed reaction. Though since Mike had offered, and I knew myself well, I did make the decision to confine our trip to the wedding day itself. Yes, it would be a long one, but the days were longer too now, so it wasn't as if we'd have to drive all the way home in the dark. Plus, Mike was right: I didn't need a Prosecco headache right now.

And I felt vindicated when I tucked Sam up in bed that night; a routine which, as is the way of such things, by now had its own unique order of events. First, a story, then a hug, then the actual tucking. Always super-tight, because Sam loved to be tightly tucked in – 'Like a sausage in a roll!'

'That's nice,' he said, when I told him he'd be going on a day trip rather than a sleepover. 'Because you're definitely the best tucker-in, *ever*.'

'I have a certificate in tucking-in,' I said as I kissed him on the forehead. 'With an actual gold star.'

He smiled sleepily at me. Then floored me completely. 'Casey,' he said, as I got up to leave the bedroom, 'you know that thing I said about calling you Mummy yesterday? So, like, people wouldn't know I wasn't your proper boy?'

'Yes, love,' I said, feeling a familiar achey feeling.

'Can I call you Mummy anyway? Just, like, for normal stuff as well?'

This, of course, was the sixty-four-million-dollar question. The local authority view – as you'd expect – was that we should tread carefully if this came up, as it was dangerous territory. Certainly, though they'd turn a blind eye, they'd never officially condone it. I also knew from personal experience; 'Mummy' is such a powerful word, after all, and for a child to ask if they can use it speaks volumes.

So, more often than not, I would happily agree to it, while pointing out, where appropriate, that the child already had a mummy, even if they weren't living with them anymore. For some kids, it was a big deal for pragmatic reasons – they'd feel less different if they could refer to you as Mum at, say, the school gate.

In others, however, it was an expression of need. They wanted to call you Mum because they felt so insecure. Because, in a time of great upheaval, it represented stability. It was also, more often than not, an expression of trust. And trust was a very precious commodity.

What to say, then? To this child who would one day all too soon be moving on from us? Though to where? Till he was fully assessed, I couldn't even guess, much less know. And right now, I was happy keeping him for myself. One thing was clear though: I wasn't his mum, nor would I ever be. Yet, how could I refuse him such a simple, heartfelt request?

With no answer to that question, I could only respond to him on instinct.

'Yes, sweetie,' I whispered. 'Of course you can.'

Chapter 20

Sam looked every inch the intrepid adventurer when we set off the next morning. He'd dressed in several layers, despite it already being warm, and accessorised his get-up with his Spider-Man backpack, and a new addition – something I'd not seen on him yet – a slightly too big *Jurassic Park* baseball cap.

'You expecting a run-in with a T-Rex, mate?' Tyler asked him, grinning, as Sam marched into the kitchen ready for the off.

'I like to be prepared,' Sam told him, his expression serious. I looked up from where I was finishing off a bit of last-minute wrapping (our wedding gift for Chloe and her fiancé having only arrived the previous day). Seeing Sam's face took me straight back to the evening he'd arrived on our doorstep, and it occurred to me that this was almost as much of a big deal for him – it would be the first time I'd left him for more than a couple of hours since he'd come to us.

'Don't forget your painting for your auntie Maureen,' I reminded him. 'Well, assuming there's any room left. What on earth have you got in there?'

'Extra clothes,' Sam told me. 'In case I get messy. And a couple of books, in case I get bored.'

'I doubt you'll have time to get bored with all the fun things I know are in store for you,' I said, 'but you're right, being prepared is always sensible. Here, tell you what, love, why don't I roll it up for you? I've got a bit of raffia ribbon here that we can tie it up with, as well.'

I rummaged in my wrappings box and found a length of discarded yellow ribbon, and between us we soon had the painting neatly tied with a bow.

'There,' I said. 'It should slide into the side pocket now.' But Sam shook his head. 'I'll carry it separately. I don't want it to get all crumpled on the journey.'

Tyler rolled his eyes. 'Mate, I *totally* feel your pain,' he said, a touch more dramatically than was strictly warranted. 'I've got to do a hundred and fifty miles in the back of Dad's car, and then spend the whole day in a horrible itchy suit. Wish I could go with you, to be honest – I reckon you're going to have a blinder of a day.'

Seeing how Sam's expression changed – that glint of hope; might Tyler be able to go with him? – I could have poked my youngest son in the ribs. In truth I was still anxious about how the day would shape up for Sam and had perhaps subconsciously braced myself, however much I'd put my doubts aside about it, for the storm clouds to gather again.

But the moment passed – not least because I made it clear, with great fuss, that Tyler couldn't 'get out of it' and must, regrettably, resign himself to a day of stultifying boredom, while Sam had a much better day in prospect, doing exactly as he pleased. And in the flurry of last-minute rushing around, there was no time to dwell on what might or might not happen. And, as it turned out, it was Sam who gave me the strongest indication that all would be well, only half an hour later.

He was quiet in the back of the car with Tyler (we were to drop him off and then drive on to pick up the motor-way from there), and completely silent from the moment we drove onto his old estate. As we all were when a pair of thirty-something ne'er-do-wells crossed the road in front of us, heads down, hoods up – drug dealers? More than likely. But as soon as we arrived, there was little doubt that he'd been telling the truth when he told me he missed Mrs Gallagher. And when she'd told me how fond she was of him, neither apparently had she.

I'd texted to say we were on our way, and she must have been looking out for us, because no sooner had we pulled up than she was out on her front doorstep and, as Sam emerged from the car, was already trotting down her front path, arms outstretched ready to embrace him.

I'd got out as well, to see Sam in, and while Mike turned the car round, I held the front gate open for him. 'Go on,' I said. 'Off you pop and say hello.' And I was heartened – bit of an understatement – to see him run towards her, and fling his arms round her neck as she scooped him up and swung him round. The affection between them was clearly mutual.

'Oh! Oh! My little darling!' Mrs Gallagher was shrieking. 'How are you, my little poppet? I'm missed you *so* much!'

In response, he hugged her tighter and, like the early-morning mist, my anxieties about the day melted away.

'Now, you two go and have a fabulous day,' Mrs Gallagher said to Mike and me, having finally put Sam down. 'Me and this little fellow will be just fine. We're going to be baking cakes and buns, and' – she was talking more to Sam than us now – 'I've even borrowed one of those DVD-thingy machines, and a film from my friend at bingo. Oh, we're going to have *such* a grand day.'

'It certainly sounds like it,' I agreed as I opened my car door again. 'We should be back here by eight o'clock latest, if that's okay? You be a good boy, Sam,' I told him, planting a kiss on his forehead.

'Oh, he's *always* a good boy, aren't you, Sam?' Mrs Gallagher answered for him.

And they were off up the path and indoors before I'd so much as clicked in my seat beat. Perhaps this *had* been a great idea, after all.

'I swear I saw tears in her eyes when she saw him,' I said to Mike as we drove away. 'God, I really feel *so* much better now.'

'Oh wonderful!' Mike said, as Tyler tittered from the back seat. 'A poor old woman sheds a tear and *that* makes you happy. Dear God, I'm married to a sadist!'

He got a punch in the arm, obviously, but it was a relaxed, happy journey. For all his protestations (which I knew were for Sam's benefit, mainly) Tyler was happy enough to plug himself in and fill the interminable journey listening to some of-the-moment podcast or other – one of his funny ones, it sounded like, because every so often he'd burst out into spontaneous laughter, for what seemed no reason at all.

Which left me free to choose my favourite digital radio station, and drive Mike half-mad singing along to it. And I felt like singing too. I'd set myself up to spend the day in a state of stress and agitation, yet since dropping Sam off, I felt none of it. In fact (though I didn't actually admit this to Mike, obviously), I half-wished I'd had the confidence to go with the original plan to stay over and collect Sam in the morning.

That wouldn't now be happening, obviously, but perhaps it was still the right thing; Sam wasn't mentally prepared for an overnight stay now in any case, even if he had packed sufficient for a month. But it certainly gave me confidence that we might do it down the line a bit, if things went as well as I hoped. The main thing, though, was that it left me free to enjoy my niece's wedding without feeling I must endlessly check my phone.

And, needless to say, the day went past in a blur. Despite Tyler's lack of enthusiasm initially – well, he was sixteen, wasn't he? – so busy was he having fun with various cousins and second cousins, that I barely saw anything of him all day. And when the time came for Mike and I to leave him in the care of the rest of the family (he was now going to be sleeping on a put-you-up in Levi and Jackson's room), it occurred to me that it would be quite a big thing for him too, as it rubber-stamped that sense that he was part of the bigger family. Not to mention the fact that the youngsters didn't need a pair of old fossils like Mike and I cramping their style.

Things were just getting under way for the evening's revelries when we left, the band setting up as we spent the obligatory half-hour saying our goodbyes. But even though we were running late, the days were now getting longer, so the sun hadn't quite set when we pulled up again at Mrs Gallagher's house.

I was really looking forward to seeing Sam again, and to an extent that surprised me. I got attached to almost all our foster kids (it kind of goes with the territory) but given that he hadn't lived with us that long, the pull he exerted was slightly unexpected. As was my insistence on us stopping at a service station on the way into town so we could buy him a bag of sweets and a can of pop as a special treat.

'Like he won't already be high on sugar from all the cakes he's been baking,' Mike quipped as we stood on the front doorstep. 'And you want to throw E numbers into the mix too? That one Prosecco must have gone to your head.'

I was just giving him a shove when the door opened and, rather than the person we'd expected – i.e. Mrs Gallagher – we found ourselves face-to-face with a giant of a man. A young man to whom I was technically more face-to-waist. He was that enormous, and I knew instinctively that it must be Mrs Gallagher's son Sean.

He had a sweet, guileless smile, and a gap between his front teeth. 'Hullo,' he said cheerfully, then raised a hand and waved to us, even though we were standing no more than a foot away from him.

'Hullo,' we parroted back in unison. 'I'm Casey and this is Mike,' I added. 'And you must be –'

'*Sean*!' I became aware of Mrs Gallagher hurrying along the hall to join us. 'Sean, love, what have I told you about answering the front door? Off you go,' she added briskly. 'Back into the lounge please, there's a good lad.' Then, to us, as her son shuffled smilingly backwards as instructed. 'I'm so sorry.' She looked and sounded flustered. 'Please do come in. This has all been a little unexpected. He wasn't supposed to be here till tomorrow morning, but one of his key workers has gone off sick, and, well … Dear me …' She waved us in and shut the door.

'It's fine,' Mike said, glancing at Sean, who was still hovering in the living-room doorway, blinking at us. 'But you must have had your hands full. I do hope Sam's been good for you.'

Mrs Gallagher placed a hand on her son's enormous chest and pushed him firmly back into the living room. 'Oh, *he's* only been back half an hour,' she said, pulling the door to and shutting it firmly. I half-expected her to call out 'Sit, and stay!' as she did so. 'Just took me by surprise, that's all, but Sam's been a little angel. We've done all kinds of things together – had the grandest time today, he has. Come on,' she added, beckoning. 'He's just out in the back garden. This way.'

She led us through the kitchen – where a wire rack of iced fairy cakes sat on the worktop – and on out through the back door, into the garden, which was as neat and well-tended close up as it had been from the bedroom window. A very far cry from Sam's old garden-in-name-only next door. I wonder how being so close to it had worked out for him.

'He's such a lovely, lovely boy,' Mrs Gallagher said as she led us out onto the dusky patio. 'And he's had a fine time, haven't you, Sam?' she added. 'Can't wait to come back, can you? Now then, here's Casey and Mike, come to take you home.'

But I knew right away that something was wrong. Because Sam wasn't listening. He was too busy counting. Sitting crossed-legged on the grass, where the lawn met the patio, counting out marbles, in rows of ten, from a big green string bag.

'Hey, Sammie boy,' Mrs Gallagher said, 'anyone in there? Look who's here for you. I told you they wouldn't be long. Didn't I promise? And here they are.'

Sam looked up now, only briefly, but long enough for me to note his drawn expression. 'Sixty-six, sixty-seven …' he said, focusing on his marbles once again.

Mrs Gallagher looked stressed, despite the smile in her voice. 'Oh, don't worry,' she said, even though neither of us had indicated that we were. 'It's just this thing of his. He'll stop counting when he gets to one hundred. Sorry,' she said again, tapping him on the shoulder to hurry him along.

I felt sorry for her. She'd obviously been sent into a spin by the unexpected arrival of her son. And off the back of what had probably been a very tiring day for her.

'Oh, it's fine,' I said. 'We already know what he's like with his counting. Don't we, Sam?' I added, smiling. But he didn't even look up at me. 'We'll just hang on till he's done, then we'll get straight off and leave you in peace. Thank you so much for doing this for us. We really appreciate it.'

'It was entirely my pleasure,' she said, but her tone didn't quite match her demeanour. It was obvious she was keen to see Sam gone as well. 'Look now,' she said to him. 'Come along now, we're all ready. Don't worry about putting them back in the bag, love,' she added. 'I'll pop them all back once you're gone.'

Now Sam did look up, but was already putting the marbles back in the bag again. And so rhythmically and intently that none of us, it seemed, felt it appropriate to try and stop him. Instead we stood and watched as all one hundred were returned to the bag. Sam stood up then and, without saying anything to anyone, simply brushed off the seat of his jeans and came and stood beside me. I was aware of his hand snaking round my back, and of him grabbing a handful of my jacket.

Feeling uneasy now, as if something fragile might explode at any moment, I decided not to prolong things, and groped for the hand so I could clasp it in my own. I then led the way back through the house, leaving Mike in my wake, and while he took possession of a selection of yet more cakes from Mrs Gallagher, I gathered up Sam's coat and bag, one-handed, in the hall.

'I have to go find something to cook for my big lump of a son now,' I heard her say, with a forced, tinkling laugh. 'Eats like a fecking horse, he does.'

'Well, there's certainly plenty of cake at least,' I heard my husband quip back. And all the while, Sam held on tightly to my hand.

I led him down the front path to the car, and opened the kerbside back door. 'Let's get you in the car, sweetie,' I said. 'You must be tired and hungry, I know we are.'

'Night, Sammy!' Mrs Gallagher called, bustling down the path to wave us off.

'I just want to go to bed,' Sam said quietly, as he climbed into the car.

'He says goodnight!' I said for him. 'And thanks again!'

And he didn't say another word all the way home, no matter how hard we tried to engage him.

True to his word, Sam didn't want any tea – though he admitted he hadn't had any. Or a bath, or a story. Just bed. 'Give him time, love,' Mike said once we'd regrouped downstairs and changed our clothes. 'I know he said he was keen to go, but we knew a part of that was because he thought it would make us happy, didn't he? In the event it was probably all a bit too much, too soon. Let's see what tomorrow brings, eh? Onwards and upwards!'

And perhaps he was right, but I couldn't see it. It felt too much like backwards and downwards. But why? What had happened? What was going through his mind? I could only hope that, come the morning, he might tell us.

Chapter 21

I'd been right. Backwards and downwards seemed to be the order of the day. So much so that, while I'd assumed Sam was just tired and anxious after his day with Mrs Gallagher (for whatever reason), when he was still pale and listless all through Sunday, I began to wonder if he was going down with some sort of bug. He was off his food, too, which made it seem even more likely.

More worrying, however, was that he seemed to be shutting down on us, barely speaking to any of us, bar monosyllabic answers, and avoiding being in any of our company. And this after a period of such intense clinginess, with me, particularly, that it felt as if I was being punished. Yet, I couldn't seem to get through to him to ask him why.

'Look, Sam,' I said, trying to get something out of him on Sunday evening. 'I put all those extra stars on your chart. Did you see? So now I need to know how you'd like to spend them. Have you any ideas yet?'

In response, I got a shrug.

'We could go out for a special dinner, or something,' I tried. 'Maybe to one of those pubs, like we went to with Colin that day. Remember the one with the play area and the ball pool? And we could ask Riley and Kieron to bring their kids along, too, so you'll have other children to play with. How about that? What do you think?'

What Sam most resembled was a child who wanted nothing more than to cry his heart out at this terrible news. 'I'm tired,' was all he said. 'Can I go and lie down?'

'It's a bit late for a lie-down, love,' I pointed out. 'It'll be bedtime in a couple of hours.'

'Can I go to bed early instead, then?'

'Okay,' I said, sighing. Perhaps we needed to leave things till the morning. 'But do try and think of something nice, sweetie, won't you? You've been so good and we want you to enjoy all the points you've earned.'

'Okay,' he said. 'I will try, I promise.'

But him fulfilling that promise showed no sign of happening when he got up, still pale and uncommunicative, the next morning.

Perhaps he did have a bug, which was compounding whatever was going on inside his head. Everything felt harder when you were physically under the weather, after all. But though he allowed me to take his temperature, when I said I was worried about him, it was normal. So he wasn't sick – well, not that kind of sick. So, what to think? And what to do?

Once again, Mike counselled that we should give it more time; that the whole episode had obviously been too much too soon. He also pointed out that, since Sam had always been a complicated child, perhaps this was just more of the same with him.

'You wait,' he reassured me when we spoke on the phone at breakfast time on Monday morning. 'Now everything's back to normal, and he knows he's safe and staying put, he'll bounce back to his old self and you'll be muttering about being careful what you wish for – specially once he's back to running around like a maniac and chucking Lego all over the house.'

But there was a feeling of doom growing in the pit of my stomach, and I couldn't seem to shake it. What *precisely* had happened? I needed to understand. I needed chapter and verse. So waiting wasn't an option – I needed to be proactive, doing something to try to fix the situation. So I decided on a strategy – to pretend that I wasn't noticing this change of behaviour. To ignore the 'go away' signals, and carry on regardless.

Starting now. I headed upstairs. 'Get dressed then, kiddo,' I said, smiling and pottering around his bedroom, straightening up various toys and books. 'Flame needs a nice long walk. He's been missing you and I promised Mrs Pegg we'd go and collect him for an hour today. So come on, chop-chop, we don't want to be late.'

I then left the room, giving him no chance to voice an objection, but hung around outside the door until I could hear evidence of him getting dressed. And thankfully, my idea bore fruit. Within minutes he was downstairs in his dog-walking get-up, but though he was with me in body, he wasn't in spirit, because though he spoke politely enough to Mrs Pegg, and made a big fuss of Flame, it was like going on a walk with a shop mannequin; a silent child who'd obviously accepted that he must accompany me but couldn't bring himself to engage in any way with me. Even Flame must have noticed the difference in his buddy's mood – where Sam was usually dashing about, throwing the ball and charging after Flame when he ran for it, today he was just like the ball-throwing doohickey – sending balls for him to fetch, like an automaton.

And when this persisted into Tuesday, and I was seriously considering taking him to the doctor's anyway, it was only the advice of Christine and Colin (both of whom I'd called with an update, and who were both confident that this would pass) that stayed my hand. He would, almost certainly, give up punishing me eventually. Because that, they both felt sure, was what he was doing. So we'd called it wrong (I noted and was grateful for that 'we'). He'd recover from it eventually, and in the meantime I mustn't worry unduly. Just let nature, not to mention the police investigation, take its course. Just keep an eye on him, etc., etc.

But perhaps they'd been right, because, finally, at Tuesday teatime, there was a breakthrough. Sam had joined us for tea, which in itself was encouraging – since returning home, he'd been avoiding eating at the same time as we did. He also wellied into his food.

'I take it you enjoyed that?' I said, smiling, as I removed his empty plate.

Sam nodded and smiled. So at least he was trying. 'It was lovely,' he said. 'Thank you. Sausage and mash and beans is my favourite.'

'That's precisely why Casey cooked it for tea, mate,' Mike said. 'And do you want to know why it's so particularly delicious?'

Sam nodded.

'It's because of her secret ingredient,' he told him. 'Before she cooks the sausages she paints them with brown sauce. Clever, huh? Any chance of seconds, love?'

I was about to tell him yes (there is never a wrong time to have extra sausages available, obviously) but Sam cleared his throat and got in first.

But he wasn't after sausages. 'I thought what I want for my stars,' he said. 'Is that okay?'

That was so out of the blue that it caught me off guard. I glanced at Mike as I picked up his plate.

'That's brilliant news,' Mike said. 'You certainly earned them, kiddo, so it's up to you. What would you like, then?'

'Would it be okay if I have some pennies for them?' Sam asked. 'Only when I was at auntie Maureen's she said it was my sister's birthday in two weeks and I want to buy her a new dolly. Is that okay?'

I almost dropped the plates. Was this what it had all been about? God, how stupid was I? I'd imagined talk of his siblings might come up when he was at Mrs Gallagher's, because how could it be avoided if he brought it up? And just because he never spoke of his brother and sister when he was with us didn't mean he wouldn't with her. And, of course, being back at home (or near enough) was bound to mean it – or, rather, *them* – would be on his mind. Bless him. Was that what all this was all about? Was it just sadness? Was it just him trying to process the reality that they were absent from his life? I made a mental note to call Mrs Gallagher in the morning and ask her what had been discussed and how it had gone. And another, to sit Sam down and properly broach it.

'Oh, sweetie,' I said, 'of *course* that's okay. And what a lovely thing to do.' Another thought then occurred to me. A bit of a wild card, since it might not be agreed to. But something told me it would. And it definitely should. This child needed to maintain a relationship with his siblings. And doing so (I was on a roll now), now he was calming down significantly, might help *all* of their emotional recovery. 'Would you like us to take you to your auntie Maureen's when your sister will be there?' I suggested. 'So you can give her the dolly yourself?'

But Sam shook his head. 'I'm not allowed to see her, so I'm gonna ask Sampson to take it to her. Can I have the pennies now to put in my special box in my room? Then maybe I can try to earn some more to go with them. I'd like to get her a nice dolly. A big one.'

'Well of course you can, darling,' I said, glancing again at Mike, who looked as surprised by this turn of events as I was. And was probably having the same thoughts. 'How much do you reckon all those stars are worth, Mike?'

Mike left his seat and made a big thing of counting up the stars on the chart from where he was sitting. 'Oh, wow,' he said, when he was done. 'I mean, there has to be five pounds' worth on there. What do you think, Ty?'

'For def,' Tyler said. He winked at Sam. 'Maybe six, even.'

I went to get my purse. 'And I imagine you could get a beautiful dolly with six pounds.' I dug out six pound coins and put them one by one in his palm, reminding him to take very good care of them.

'I'll put them straight in my box now,' he said, 'and I'll guard them with some of my fireman trucks. Can I stay in my room and watch telly now, please?'

I don't know what had brought on the breakthrough, but I was over the moon. Perhaps he'd just needed that couple of days to process his feelings. And had come to the conclusion that he could do something tangible to make amends for what had happened before. I didn't know how his brother and sister spoke about him now – how they felt about their older brother – but I made another mental note: to find out. For the moment, though, I was just happy at this positive turn of events. Perhaps spending time with Mrs Gallagher had been the right thing after all. Perhaps it would prove to have been a key step on the road to healing. Even re-establishing contact, which I was even more determined to push for.

'See,' Mike said, grinning, once Sam had left the room. 'I told you it would be okay, didn't I?'

* * *

I had agreed that it might, and when I got up the next morning, I felt the same rush of optimism for Sam. There were many hurdles to jump still – not least, a second police interview – but this must surely open up a dialogue I was very keen to have and the re-establishment of some foundations for him.

It was in that mood that I started my day. Why wait for the weekend? Why not take Sam out shopping today? Starting with another special breakfast at my sister's café. So, having seen Mike and Tyler off – both were out of the door at half past seven – I immediately headed upstairs to wake Sam up with a glass of milk, and to tell him about my – *our* – exciting plans.

'Morning, sleepyhead!' I called as I walked over to his bed. 'Time to get up and washed and dressed. Guess where we're going this morning?'

There was no reply. And no movement to indicate that he was awake. I put the milk on his bedside table and jiggled the mound under the duvet. It was then – in that instant – that the terrible truth dawned. I'd pressed down not on Sam, but on something softer and squidgier. And even as I whipped the duvet back and saw the pillows, I already knew. He'd outfoxed us all: he'd run away.

Chapter 22

Forget aqua aerobics. I should have spent my time doing yoga. Because as I dashed about, gathering evidence that Sam had done as I feared, I could have done with a yogic chant or two to help calm me down. Coat, boots, and baseball cap. Some items of clothing. The Spider-Man backpack. Two of the nests of counting things from the bottom of his chest of drawers. Plus the money from his pot, of course. That precious six pounds.

I dressed in a hurry, cursing myself for not having considered it. For being so blinded by my conviction that Sam's 'thing' was to cling to me, I had never once considered what should surely have been staring me in the face. That Sam no longer trusted us to take sufficient care of him, to keep him safe, and had laid plans to take care of himself. No wonder he'd been so quiet and reluctant to communicate. He'd been too busy working out how.

I pulled a jacket on, grabbed my keys and phone, gulped down the last of my cold coffee and walked down to Mrs Pegg's anyway. Despite the evidence to the contrary, there was still a slim chance that he'd simply decided to take Flame on a very early walk.

He had certainly, as I'd half-feared, taken Flame.

'No, he's – *what*?' Mrs Pegg's expression responded to my own straight away. 'What's happened? What's the matter? He's gone to walk him. I thought you *were* him, bringing him back. Didn't you *know*?'

I couldn't lie to her. 'No, I didn't. I thought he was still in bed. Did he say anything to you?'

'I thought it was rather early,' she answered. 'But he said he had to walk him early because you and he were going out for the day. Oh God! Where's he taken him?'

I could sense her rising panic. 'Just to the park, I imagine,' I said firmly. 'I'll head there now. I'm sure everything is going to be okay.'

She looked at her watch. 'But he had his backpack. And he's already been gone over an hour,' she said. 'Well over.'

I did some maths. So he'd snuck out before Mike had gone downstairs.

'I'm sure I'll find him,' I told her. I didn't know what else to say. 'He'll be down in the park, or the woods, I'm sure of it. He won't have gone far. He's just ...' I stopped. This was no time for speculation or explanation. 'Please try not to worry,' I said instead. 'He loves Flame. He wouldn't hurt him in a million years. I know he wouldn't.'

'I'm not worried about that,' Mrs Pegg said. She had an edge to her voice now. 'He's *nine*, Casey. He's the one I'm worried about most.'

Duly chastised, I set off for the park, more in hope than expectation. And on the way, I phoned Christine, who immediately told me to log it with EDT – 'in case you don't find him,' she added ominously, 'and the police need to be involved'. But as she was in a traffic jam on the way to work, and the cars had started moving, she then had to ring off again, and could only promise to call me back as soon as she got there.

I promised I would call EDT, but my instinct was first to call Colin. Hadn't he said he'd taken Sam to some 'special place' when they'd gone on their adventure? Where had that been? Was it walkable? If so, perhaps he'd gone there? Colin confirmed that it was, well, at least, just about, if Sam could remember the way. And since Sam didn't know the area, and had proved himself to be a planner, it seemed my best course of action would be to get my car and head there.

'So can you give me directions?' I asked Colin.

'Wait for me,' he said instead. 'I'm only twenty minutes away from you. I'll head there right away.'

Since I was already in the park now, I did a circuit of it anyway. And since others were too, I asked three people if they'd by any chance seen Sam and Flame. No one had, as I now expected, because the reality was sinking in now. If Sam's intention was to leave us, why on earth would he go there? But why take the dog?

For protection, Casey. Get with the frigging programme. Plus a few scraps of clothing, and the six pounds we'd given him. To start the fantasy life he'd already sketched out to me – to live in a big, golden castle on a hill, wasn't it? And have a dog just like Flame, to protect him from all the bad men who lived in the woods.

Did he really think six pounds would be enough to start a new life together? Possibly. How would he have any sort of real grasp of money? What *I* grasped, however, was the extent of his planning. He at least knew he'd need money, hence all the stuff about the dolly. Which made me wonder anew about what had happened at Mrs Gallagher's. Perhaps his little sister hadn't even been discussed. Perhaps Sam had come up with that all on his own, to throw me off-track so that he could implement his plan. It had worked.

Colin was already parked outside when I ran back up my street towards home. And I wasted no time going indoors. Simply jumped into his car and, as we set off again, ran through the events of the last twenty-four hours with him.

'Sold us all a dummy, then,' Colin observed as we headed off down a lane.

'Or perhaps we're the ones who were the dummies here,' I told him.

It wasn't a long drive. No more than ten minutes had passed before Colin indicated, and pulled off the lane onto land that I'd passed many times. But that still represented a substantial walk for a small boy.

We'd pulled in at an opening between two high beech hedges, now dense with their distinctive lime-green spring finery. I recognised it but, had I not, the council had kindly provided information – former wasteland, that had once been the grounds of a ruined country house, it was in the process of being turned into, or at least heralded as, a 'a place of natural beauty'. A stream had been uncovered during the ground working stages and the photographs on the surrounding billboards depicted it, bubbling gaily, surrounded by sculptured greenery, an 'eco' visitor centre, various benches, and a picnic area, complete with brick barbecues, all set among pretty glades of mature trees. It was a picture of serenity that was so perfect and idealised that it couldn't help but grate against my current state of mind.

'In here?' I asked. 'You took him into the building site? Were you allowed to?'

'No, Casey, not the building site,' Colin explained as we continued to drive, now down a tree-lined dirt track. 'There's no building going on yet, not that I can see, anyway. Though there could be elsewhere,' he said, as we suddenly emerged into the light again, now in what looked like the grounds of the house that once stood there. All I could see was a low fenced-off ruin, and further away, unfenced, the remains of a couple of outbuildings.

'There,' Colin said, pointing. 'That's where I brought him. Fifty pence says he's somewhere in there.'

I realised that a part of him was enjoying our small adventure. Which at first I mentally berated him for, but then did a backtrack. This, after all, was the side of his job that knocked the hours in the office, form-filling, into a cocked hat. Till such time as he seriously believed Sam was lost and in danger, why on earth wouldn't he enjoy it? Or, if 'enjoy' wasn't the right word, then at least find it a bit thrilling. And that he would find him here, he seemed to be in no doubt.

He parked up just by the fence that bordered the house itself, a short walk from the outbuildings, which could only be reached by ground too rough and lumpy to risk taking the car. 'Over there,' he said, nodding straight ahead, towards a big old shed, as he yanked up the hand-brake. 'That's where we holed up for a bit and hid' – he smiled sheepishly, but not that sheepishly – 'in case there were any dark forces hunting for us.'

I arched my eyebrows and shook my head – his confidence was contagious. And it did seem a very likely place for Sam to run off to hide in.

'Fingers crossed, then,' I said, climbing out of the car, and stepping down onto muddy mush, grateful that I'd chosen trainers over sandals.

'I know this place,' I told Colin and I joined him in traversing the rough ground that separated us from the huddle of sheds and barns. 'This land was turned over to allotments for a while years ago – look, you can still see the odd leek sprouting up. My dad had one for a bit. There's a stream just behind. I used to come down with a bucket and fill his water butt from it. I think at one stage it was privately owned, but they never managed to get planning permission. I think it's just been left to rot since. I didn't even know you could still get to it.'

'I doubt you could,' Colin said. 'Not till the council bought it back, anyway. And it's good that it's going to be developed into a park now, rather than yet another sprawling all-too-soon-to-be-grim sink estate.'

For a moment, I was surprised that someone so young could have such strong opinions about local town-planning decisions. But I checked myself. Of course he would. He was a social worker, wasn't he? So he knew more about such things than many of his age. Saw rather too much about what 'sink', in this case, meant.

It also reminded me – and him too, I think – why we were there. To find a boy who wanted only to live somewhere better, somewhere safer, even if it was a landscape that existed only in his imagination.

And he was here. I knew immediately, because we suddenly heard 'woof!'. And a dog woof, rather than a boy's woof. I was certain it must be Flame, who'd heard us coming. And though this was immediately followed by 'shh!' – this definitely human – within a minute we had come around the back of the largest of the sheds, to find both boy and dog, sitting by the stream.

'There,' I whispered. 'Do you think he'll run off if we shout to him?'

'I doubt it,' Colin said. 'We've effectively cut him off. Unless he makes a break via the water, that is.'

I felt the tension leave my shoulders. Felt them slide down a little. But, in its place came a great rush of compassion. Sam cut such a forlorn figure, sitting cross-legged on the ground, with one arm round Flame's shoulder, keeping him close. As if Flame wouldn't want to be close; he was a dog after all. And Sam now his 'pack', who he knew to keep safe.

'Come on,' said Colin. 'Let's just go and say hello, shall we?'

And as we hiked across the once-tended ground – full now of ant hills, earth and rubble – Sam heard us, then saw us, but, thankfully, didn't bolt. Perhaps because he knew us, perhaps because he deemed it pointless. Perhaps because, and this seemed likely, given how far he'd come, he was just too exhausted.

'Oh, sweetheart, I've been so worried,' I said as we approached. 'You've had us worried sick. How are you doing? You okay?'

I crouched down beside him. Though Colin had more practical help to offer. 'Here,' he said, producing a paper bag from his jacket pocket. 'Half a steak slice. Still warm. Go on, get that down you.'

Sam took it, uncurled the bag and inspected the contents. Then took the pastry from the bag and divided it in two, giving half to Flame, who fell upon it with much happy tail-wagging as Sam began nibbling the edge of his half.

To say I was moved would be like saying Riley was 'slightly pleased' last year, when, after six months of dieting, she managed to get into her old prom dress.

I therefore took Colin's cue and sat as Sam was, cross-legged, and we waited for him to eat his impromptu breakfast before trying to get him to speak.

It didn't take long, but there were many crumbs, which he seemed anxious to deal with first. Only then did I attempt to engage him.

'Sam, sweetheart,' I said once he was done, 'what's all this about, love? Can you tell us?'

I could see he'd been crying, but he was resolutely dry-eyed now, as if he'd tried crying on for size enough to know it was pointless. 'Sam?' I tried again. 'Sam, it has to be something. Is it the bad man you're scared of? If you don't tell us, love, we can't help you, can we?'

Sam looked straight at me. 'You can't help me. No one can. I *told* you.'

'But sweetheart, we can. We *are*. I told you. You're safe now. Me and Colin –'

'No I'm not!' his voice was shrill now. 'You sent me back there!'

I reached out a hand to him, but Flame intercepted it, and licked it. *Keep going, Casey*, it seemed to say. *You'll get there.*

'I didn't, sweetie. Honest. Yes, I took you to your auntie Maureen's and I know you found that difficult. And if I'd had half a brain cell I'd have never let you go there. Not when it's made you so frightened and upset again. That was the very last thing I wanted. But –'

A hand on my shoulder stopped me. It was Colin's. Reaching across from his end of the powwow. 'Sam,' he said, touching his own temple, 'I think I'm getting something now, from my superhero senses. Sam, tell me, if you can. The bad man. Is it Sean?'

235

Comprehension had dawned even before Colin said the name. Dawned even before his hand had touched my shoulder. Perhaps I had superhero senses too.

And perhaps I needed to listen to them better.

Oh God. All this time. All this long, long *time*. Sean. If I'd been the sort to swear, I would have sworn now, no question.

But it was as if I wasn't even there.

Sam nodded at Colin. Fixed his gaze on him, and only him. 'So will you help me? You need to help me. We need to kill him.'

Chapter 23

By the time we got Sam back home, he seemed to have gone into shock. It might have been partly because of the long scary walk, in a place he didn't know well, in the early-morning air – not to mention the nature of what he'd planned to do. But my hunch was that it was more likely fear. Fear of having run away with my neighbour's dog, and what consequences that might mean for him. Fear also of the consequences of having finally divulged his secret. If so, he had taken on board what I'd taught him about consequences, and how terrible an irony was that?

While I took Sam back indoors, Colin ran up the road to return Flame to Mrs Pegg – no worse, and perhaps better, for his unscheduled adventure. He'd bounced around excitedly in the back of Colin's car on the way home – like the puppy he'd not been in a long time. So at least one of the duo had had their best morning ever, then, I thought ruefully. And I could tell by the way Sam kept absently stroking him that Flame had and would continue to play a big part in helping Sam to cope. Well, as long as Mrs Pegg would let him.

I helped Sam off with his coat (he was white as a sheet now, and shaking, and I suspected he might well be sick, too) and his backpack, which – unsurprisingly – weighed a ton. 'Goodness, you packed for every eventuality then!' I quipped, hoping to help hold him together by keeping things light. But, to my consternation, he burst into sudden, racking sobs.

'I'm sorry,' he cried, burying his face against my middle. 'I'm sorry, I didn't mean to take them. Honest, I didn't! Honest! I just thought just in case!'

'What's all this about?' I said, pulling back a little so I could see his face. But he wasn't having any of it, and refused to move his head.

'Shhh,' I soothed, wondering what the 'them' referred to. What things he might need 'just in case'. But, right now, that wasn't important. 'It's okay, Sam,' I said. 'Shush, now. Let's get you sat down before you fall down. Come on. Into the living room. Colin will be back in just a moment. Don't worry, okay? Everything is going to be alright now, I promise.'

Even as I said it, I realised how empty my promises must sound. Me – his trusted carer – who had misinterpreted everything, and instead of being the protector I was meant to be – and thought I'd been – had unknowingly sent him straight into the lion's den. It still beggared belief. Yet now he'd said it, it made sense. Perfect sense, in fact, which made the fact that I'd been blind to it almost incomprehensible.

But perhaps I'd been as guilty of stereotyping as the next person – Sean Gallagher had been presented to me as a big friendly bear character; an innocent, a gentle child in a too-big adult body. Perhaps the very last person you'd associate with sexual abuse. But I knew better. As I should. I was trained to know better. Yet so readily had I been primed to accept the alternative narrative (not least because I'd had run-ins with more abusive drug dealers than I cared to remember) that I'd ceased to think critically and just accepted it.

But there would be time enough for soul-searching and dissecting everything later. In the here and now we needed Sam to tell us everything he could. And just as I'd sat Sam down on the sofa, having helped him out of his muddy trainers, I heard the sound of the front door closing. Colin appeared in the living-room doorway moments later.

'Mrs Pegg sends her love, mate,' he said to Sam immediately. 'She said not to worry about Flame, okay? She said she knew you'd take care of him and is glad you've tired him out for her.' He took off his jacket. 'Anyway, alright? How you doing? Bearing up?'

Sam nodded. Colin's return seemed to perk him up a little. Well, in truth, perk him up a *lot*. Because once his fellow superhero sat down in the armchair opposite, it was as if Sam was a dam with the finger plucked out.

And as I listened to his stream of words – of the bad man and how he'd tricked him, and how he'd made him do things he didn't want to, and how he dare not tell anyone, *ever*, or he'd hurt him more – I knew two things for sure. The first was that there was no question that Sam was telling us the truth, and the second was that I hoped it wasn't exhausting him too much because I knew he would have to tell it at least once again and, much more likely, more than once. To strangers.

Which made it seem doubly important that he deal with as much as he could today so, under cover of making us all drinks and getting biscuits, I slipped out into the garden, to phone Kim Dearing and ask if she, or someone else, could come round and see him here, now, today.

Ideally her, though. Even though I knew she might not be on duty. But, happily, she answered her mobile at the first ring.

'Is there any way you could get over here?' I asked, once I'd given her the gist. 'I know you're probably up to your eyes, but I'd really love it if we can strike while the iron's hot. Not give him too much time to think and get frightened all over again. I'm also all too aware that this whole thing could drag on for ages and if the hard part could be done now – as in you taking his official statement – he'll at least have got the worst of it out of the way.'

'Oh, the poor lad,' Kim said. 'But your timing is good, at least. I can be with you within the hour. Though if it goes to court now and, from what you've told me, it might well do, there's obviously going to be more of the same down the line.'

'That's okay,' I said. 'We can cross that bridge when we come to it. It would just be great if he can get this bit done and we can put it behind us. And at least we know who the perpetrator is, so that should help.'

'Well, in theory,' Kim said. 'Not sure it'll speed things up any.'

'But won't he be arrested?'

'Probably,' Kim said, 'but just for questioning, initially. There has to be evidence and, without an admission, getting that can be a pretty lengthy process. But don't worry about that now. I'll make some calls and I'll be over. Case of one step at a time, at least for the moment.'

Rather than huffing and puffing in frustration – which I felt like doing, because I knew what a protracted business was probably ahead of us – I took a few deep breaths after hanging up the phone. I knew it was just the inevitable response to the situation, because my rational self knew that in cases like this it was never as simple as a child pointing the finger at someone and then everything being cut and dry, and – abracadabra – the bad man goes directly to jail.

In real life, children told lies. Or, to use the modern jargon, 'alternative truths'. Especially children who'd had traumatic childhoods. In real life, there were children who were so messed up inside that they made wild, false allegations simply to get their own way. I'd seen and heard it myself, hadn't I? More than once.

But in this case, I just knew that that *wasn't* the case. That Sam was telling the truth, which made me feel bad

241

all over again, because we'd literally handed him over, into the arms of a monster. No, not for long, and I had no evidence that they'd even interacted, but he'd *been there*, for a bit, at least, and just the fact of him being there must have been terrifying for Sam.

I returned to the living room, where Colin was showing Sam something on his phone. Some YouTube video or other – presumably to try and distract him. And now I had to break the news to him that the ordeal wasn't yet over. That he had to tell it all to the policewoman he'd met before, as well.

His face crumpled and I hugged him on the sofa as he cried.

'You remember how important she is, sweetheart?' I reminded him. 'I know it's *so* hard to tell, but you've done the big job now. You've told me and Sampson and that was really, really brave. But the trouble is that, though Sampson is a superhero, obviously, we aren't in the police, which means we can't do anything yet. Whereas Kim can arrest him and help fix things for you. She just has to know the story like we do, okay?'

'Exactly. You're *such* a brave boy, Sam,' Colin added, reaching into his shoulder bag and pulling out a hard-backed A4 notebook. 'So d'you know what I'm going to do while we wait for Kim to get here? I'm going to draw a picture of you in my special pad – a portrait of you, yes? So I never forget what a real-life superhero looks like.'

I was utterly bemused. What an idiosyncratic and brilliant diversion. I made a mental note to add it to my armoury of skills right away. I was then impressed, as Colin flicked through to find a blank page to draw on, to see that it was indeed a special pad, as opposed to a pad he was just calling special, full of sketches and drawings that were really detailed and masterful – the kind you might expect from a fan of Marvel heroes and comic books.

Colin then took a well-used pencil from an inside pocket, licked the end of the lead and began to draw. Though not for long. He put the pad down and, as we both craned our necks to see what he'd done, re-sited himself cross-legged on the floor, all the better to capture Sam's 'heroic profile'.

And that's how we still were when Kim Dearing arrived, fifty-odd minutes later.

I went to let her in, and asked if we could stay like that too. 'You know, sitting in the living room, informally, as we are?'

'Of course,' Kim said. 'Did you prime him that I was coming?'

I nodded. 'Well, as well as I could, of course. It won't be easy for him to go through it again, obviously.'

'We'll be fine,' she said, before following me back into the room, where she acknowledged Colin, and took the armchair he'd vacated.

'Hello, Sam,' she said. 'I hear that you've been the bravest little boy ever this morning! You collected the dog, went for a long walk to do your *very best* thinking, and then you decided to do a very scary, very courageous thing – am I right?'

Sam scrubbed at his eyes before looking across at Kim. 'I told them the truth. But now you have to go get Sean, because he might kill auntie Maureen.'

'He won't, Sam,' Kim reassured him. 'He absolutely won't, and, anyway, it's okay because you will never have to worry about that again. Someone will take Sean away so that *everybody* is safe, okay? Now, I know you've told Casey and Colin, but now you need to tell me. Can you do that? Can you tell me again what Sean did to you?'

'He hurt me. He hurt my winkie.'

'Okay,' she said, writing. 'When was this, Sam? When did he first hurt you?'

Sam thought. 'It was after we made friends. A bit after that. He gave me chocolate biscuits when Mummy forgot we were hungry. He said it was a proper game, like Lego and colouring in.'

'Your brother and sister too? He gave them food? Played games with them?'

Sam nodded. 'He gave them food, but he never played with them, like we did. He said they were babies and babies were tell-tales. He said he only wanted to play with me because I was a big boy.'

'Did you tell him not to touch you? Did you say you would tell your mummy?'

'I did, but it was no good because Sean was very big. He said he would choke my little sister and kill her if I told on him.'

'Did you stop wanting to be friends then?'

Sam frowned. 'Yes. But I couldn't. He said if I did he

would grab me from my bed one night and take me far away where no one would ever find me.'

Sam had begun crying again, but still Kim pressed on.

'How old were you, Sam, when Sean started hurting you?'

Sam extended an arm and let his hand hover in the air. 'This big,' he said. 'Only little. It was for ages.'

'And did he hurt you only when you slept at auntie Maureen's, or did he come to your house and hurt you there too?'

'At first it was just at their house, but when I told Mummy I didn't want to sleep there any more, he came round so he could hurt me at my house instead.'

'And where were Mummy and your sister and brother when this happened?'

'They weren't there.'

'I understand that, but where might they have been? Did you know?'

Sam seemed to find this hard to answer. Then it seemed to make sense to him. 'He came when I was in bed. I was sent to bed a lot.' He glanced at me here. 'When I was naughty. Mummy let him come up to my room because he brought me buns and biscuits. She didn't –'

He stopped, but I could provide the end of the sentence for him – either with 'know', which perhaps she wouldn't have. Or 'care'.

'Sam, this is important,' Kim said. 'So you must think hard before you answer. Did you ever tell Mummy that Sean was doing things to you?'

An emphatic head shake, followed by a broken sob. 'I never.'

'Can you tell me why, Sam?'

'I nearly. Once I told him I would tell. But he'd made me touch his winkie too. And –' he touched his tongue. I winced. 'And he said I was a *really* bad boy for doing that and, if Mummy found out, I would go to kids' jail forever and never see anyone again.'

This simple explanation – he'd not articulated this before – made me want to alternately weep, and to punch something, hard. And there was more, too. The mystery of the dog cage. Apparently it had indeed started out as a one-time punishment. Sam had hit his little sister and his mum had called him an animal, and had dragged him out into the garden and thrown him in the cage, where she'd told him he could stay till he was sorry. She'd drawn the bolt across, but hadn't bothered with the key and padlock that was looped through the wire. Sam had though, and before long had squirrelled it away, realising that if he could lock *himself* in there it could become a sanctuary from Sean.

'He wouldn't dare try and get me out of there,' Sam said, 'because people would be able to see him.' Not least his own mother, I thought, from her upstairs windows.

So it was that the cage became Sam's safe place. He soon took to locking himself in there on an almost daily basis, and when his brother or sister would come out to giggle at him being in there, he would bark and howl and pretend to be a dog to make them laugh – or, as time went on, to go away. He would also beg his mum to use the cage as a punishment rather than sending him to bed because he knew Sean dare not try anything when he was in there.

'Can I ask a question, love?' I asked, glancing at Kim, who nodded. 'Was Sean around all the time? Or just sometimes? I thought he lived away.'

'Not then,' Sam said. 'That only happened a little while ago.'

Kim noted this. 'And now I have another question for you, Sam. Another very important one. And my last one, because then we'll be finished. So I want you to think hard about this one, okay? Did you ever tell your auntie Maureen about what Sean did? Did she know?'

Sam nodded immediately. 'I never told her though,' he added, anxiously.

'I understand that,' Kim said. 'But how do *you* think she knew?'

'Because she saw. And after that she helped me.'

'She helped you? Did she tell someone for you?'

Now he shrugged. 'I don't know.'

'So how did she help you?'

'One time I slept there. This was before I lived in the dog cage.' *Lived* in the dog cage. *Oh*, *my*, I thought, *oh, my*.

'Slept at your auntie Maureen's?'

'Yes. She'd make us up beds on her settees.'

'And what happened?'

'Sean used to sneak down and take me up to his bedroom,' Sam said. 'And one night I cried, and she heard me, and she found me.'

'Found you in Sean's bed?'

Sam's tears were falling in an unbroken stream now. A sniff. Another nod. 'Sean was touching my winkie and auntie Maureen screamed at him and hit him lots of times. Then she took me off him and carried me into her bed instead.'

'And what did she say to you, Sam? When she did that?'

'She said I'd had a *really* bad dream. And that she would always look after me. And I could sleep in her bed all the time if I wanted.'

'But you didn't.'

'No, I wanted to, but I felt safer in the dog cage. Till he left.'

'You mean when he went away? When Sean went away?'

'Yes. For most of the time he didn't live there anymore. And when he wasn't there I went round to auntie Maureen's. Auntie Maureen was nice. She didn't hurt me. Not ever. She said she loved me.'

'And did she speak to you again, about the things Sean had done to you?'

'No, she said I mustn't think of it. That it would make me feel sad if I did. She told me to do the counting thing instead.'

'The counting thing?'

'Sam counts things up to a hundred,' I explained.

'She said if I ever had a bad thought, I shouldn't say anything about it. Because if I said about it to anyone, it would make it grow bigger in my head. She said I should just count things like cornflakes, or buttons, or beads. And when I got to a hundred the bad thoughts would go away again.'

'And would they?' Kim asked.

'Only sometimes. Not really.'

I felt numb. Completely poleaxed. And had two burning questions.

Was Maureen Gallagher complicit in her son's activities?

Her son who was brain-damaged, moreover, so, however awful his actions, was not – could not be – wholly responsible for what he'd done. What did that make her? Was she the real monster here?

Chapter 24

The word 'transformational' should not be used lightly, especially where troubled children are concerned. Yes, it's true that professional interventions can be transformative. It was certainly transformative for Sam and his siblings to have been taken into care. Had they not been, who knows how much lower they would have sunk? How much more neglect and abuse might have been their lot? And, had they not been removed, how much wider would have been the ripples, as damaged children ended up becoming damaged adults?

But mending children's hearts and minds rarely happened in such a way. Where superheroes could use their powers to effect striking, instant change, us mere mortals had to content ourselves with slower, less dramatic progress. A little here, a little there. Sometimes seemingly endless plateaus. Which was why patience was a virtue we all had to aspire to, as well as determination when the inevitable 'one step forward, two steps back' hiccups happened.

But sharing his secret was, for Sam, transformational. And in immediate, measurable ways.

For starters, that evening, wrung out and exhausted as he was, he surprised me by bringing down from his bedroom all the little collections of things he'd been using for his counting, declaring that he didn't need to count things anymore. So back went all the Lego, to the box in the living room, the buttons I'd given him, the sequins, the pebbles and the beans. There were other collections too, of little scraps of torn paper, of beads from his bean-bag – extracted from a tiny hole he'd made in one of the seams, and even an unfinished collection of bottle tops, which I presumed he'd purloined from the recycling.

He slept soundly that night, and woke cheerfully in the morning. It's a cliché, the old term to 'put it behind you', but Sam seemed to be a prime example of doing exactly that. Unburdened now, he seemed to be looking only forward, able to do so because he was at last free of the fear that had been dogging him for so long.

Which meant he trusted – despite everything, he appeared again to trust us. Me, despite my error of judgement in sending him back to Mrs Gallagher, and Colin – forget superheroes, there was common or garden hero-worship there – and Kim Dearing, who had clearly managed to convince him that she'd taken charge now and would make everything alright.

I decided not to mention my discoveries in his back-pack. Grabbing the opportunity, when seeing Kim out, while Colin was completing Sam's drawing, I'd had a rummage and beneath the various small items of what he'd deemed to be essential clothing (the Fireman Sam pyjamas being one such) I'd found my vegetable knife, a ball of string, my jacket potato skewer and a tiny hammer that had come with a block of toffee. Two Christmasses back, if I remembered rightly.

Items of self-defence, I deduced, with a pang of self-recrimination. While we'd gone off to enjoy our wedding, he'd gone to the Gallaghers armed, 'just in case' of attack. I took them all out and put them back where they lived. The least said about any of it, I reckoned, the better.

But while Sam seemed to be thriving, having addressed and voiced his demons, they'd come and invaded my mind instead. So I was itching to get things moving on, moving forwards. Seeing progress in the business of getting Sam sorted. Though at the same time I knew there was a long way to go; not only along the road of the impending police investigation and court case, but also the business of finding Sam a school as soon as possible, which depended on getting that all-important assessment done.

As everyone who knows me can testify, I want all that kind of thing dealt with as soon as it's mentioned. I hate having a ton of red tape to cut through – hate having mountains to climb before anything gets done. But, that being so, I'd clearly chosen the wrong career. Nothing to do with the welfare of looked-after children happens quickly. And quite rightly. It's right that due process is followed, because life-changing decisions are involved and should never be taken lightly. But there's another reason – money and its bed-fellow, lack of resources. Which meant there were queues and waiting lists for everything and anything you might need to support and help a child on their way. Sam would have to take his place on them and there was diddly-squat I could do about it.

So I was as stunned as I was excited when, just over two weeks after Sam had made his allegations, Christine Bolton phoned me to say that she needed to come and visit me to discuss strategy and plans for his long-term future.

'At last!' I enthused. 'Honestly, Christine, I couldn't be happier, and Sam will be over the moon. He's getting rather settled at home – a little too settled, if you know what I mean – and I'd hate for him to lose his enthusiasm for school at this stage.'

'Well, best you not say anything yet, Casey,' Christine warned. 'You know how things can suddenly change in this game. And might well do in this case,' she added mysteriously. 'I also have an update on Maureen and Sean Gallagher for you, so it might be best if you could ensure that Sam isn't in when I come. I know Colin will be happy to take him out, if that's going to a problem for you, and if he isn't free I can get one of our pool workers to come across and take him out somewhere instead. When is likely to suit you anyway? I'm fairly free the rest of this week if you are.'

As if I wouldn't be, I thought, smiling to myself. My diary had just the one repeat entry in it – caring for Sam.

Which, now he was free of the dark secret he'd been harbouring, I was seeing the benefits of more every day. But which didn't mean *he* would benefit from being with me *all* day and *every* day. There was life to be had outside our house, and he needed to go and live it. 'That should be fine,' I said. 'Let me just check with Kieron when he has his day off this week, and we'll see if we can arrange it for then.' I promised to phone her straight back.

So it was that two days later, when Christine arrived for our meeting, Sam and Kieron had already left for a nearby football pitch, complete with a football and goalie gloves, so he could have a bit of coaching, and a thrown-together picnic for lunch. A picnic which included a brace of home-made flapjacks, made by myself, along with Sam, the new sous chef.

I laid out some now. And a big pot of tea for her, as was now the routine, Christine being the person for whom the phrase 'all the tea in China' was made for. I wouldn't have been surprised if she'd told me that to get through the night she had tea infused into her veins.

She gave me an update on her father-in-law, for whom they hoped they'd found a home now, and we'd naturally gone on to discuss our respective families, and Chloe's wedding – which seemed like a lifetime ago now. So she was onto her second mugful by the time we got to the meat of the matter – Sam's future – but first there was the story she had to tell about Maureen Gallagher, who had been on my mind, day and night, since the day of Sam's disclosures, and become, in my imagination, some kind of she-devil. I just couldn't get my head around the idea that she'd acted as she had – i.e. *not* acted – on such a terrible discovery. Wouldn't any normal person have said something? *Done* something?

I suppose I was hoping Christine would tell me something in mitigation; something that would allow me to forgive her.

'She has been honest with us about everything,' Christine told me. 'Extremely honest. In fact, so honest that it will probably be to her detriment.'

It turned out that Sam had been correct in saying that the night Maureen found him in Sean's bed was the first time she realised what had been going on. Yes, she'd had her suspicions that Sean was 'sexually active', and interested in the sensations of sexual arousal – she'd found one of her old mail-order catalogues hidden under his bed, and had 'put two and two together'. But she'd never thought for a moment that he'd 'do anything' with it. For one thing, he barely interacted with anyone apart from her – only the carers at the day centre she took him to then, which was obviously a very public environment.

And it had never crossed her mind that he'd think to 'prey' on innocent children. Which was why, when she found Sam in bed with him that night, she had been horrified, repulsed, appalled and very angry. And she had indeed attacked him, quite brutally. She'd also, at that point, resolved to tell someone about it, perhaps the day centre, to ask for their advice.

But with morning had come an appreciation of the probable consequences. If she shared what she'd seen, let alone reported it to the authorities, she would be responsible for putting her brain-damaged, vulnerable son in a prison cell for years, wouldn't she? She would also lose her relationship with the children from next door for good – something that she couldn't bear to think about. So she decided to deal with it another way.

'And that's when she started badgering the authorities on a daily basis for Sean to have full-time residential care,' Christine said. 'She told them he'd become violent towards her and that she feared for her life. And that financially, too, she could no longer cope – the burden was just becoming too much. That's not true, by the way,' Christine added. 'She owns her home and after her husband died – some years back, by all accounts – she got a pay-out from a substantial life assurance policy.'

'Still,' I said, my feelings wavering from one moment to the next, 'it still meant that she wasn't taking any responsibility for what happened to poor Sam. However she paints it, she was wrong, and has possibly scarred the boy for life. All that talk of counting, and keeping quiet, so it didn't get out. Gagging him, in effect, which has clearly put him under enormous mental strain. If she cared for him – all of them – how could she not see that was wrong? And what's to stop Sean from reoffending if he doesn't even know he's offended?'

I hadn't been made aware of any prosecutions as yet, so I didn't know what stage things were at in that regard. I had tried to ask, and though Kim had promised she'd tell me when there was news, I got the impression that those in charge were keeping me out of the loop. Working on a strict 'need to know' basis, I guessed, and as it was no longer at my door, I probably wouldn't find out until it was all over. One of the many frustrating aspects of fostering 'protocol'.

'Well, that's the thing,' Christine said. 'Sean was still taken to the police station and questioned, despite the level of his understanding. But it won't go much further now – certainly not to court, because of his lack of capacity – but he does know he's done something very bad, and he's been taken from the facility he's been living at and moved to a secure unit for adults with severe learning disabilities.'

Good for Sam's peace of mind, obviously, but something else occurred to me. 'But won't the other residents be at risk from him?'

'It's a proper secure unit, Casey. That means locked doors, single rooms, twenty-four-hour supervision. I don't think he'll ever be able to hurt anyone ever again. I feel for him, to be honest. Don't you? I suppose the only positive is that his disability is such that "locked up forever more" isn't something that computes.'

Christine was right. It was chilling to think about. And I did feel for him, because however limited his understanding, he would surely feel the stress of having been taken away from all that was familiar. Not so different from Sam and his brother and sister, really. You'd need a hard heart not to sympathise in such a dreadful set of circumstances.

'And what about Maureen?' I asked. 'Is she being charged with anything?'

Christine shrugged. 'Now that I'm not entirely sure about. The police are still considering what to do there, so they tell me. She was complicit, and doesn't deny that she'd been so for many months, but, in her defence, she did take immediate steps to try and keep Sam safe. Well, from her own son, at least, which was obviously her main priority. And though everything she said was true – about the squalor next door, and the mother's mental state, and kids' neglect – she doesn't deny that one of her reasons for finally calling social services was that she was fearful, with Sam particularly, that, with his own mental state deteriorating, it might all come out. That – and this is key, given that we fostered them separately in part due to what she'd told us – he might confide in his brother and sister. She was also becoming anxious about it happening again – though her son was now in residential care there was always the worry that something might happen when he came home to visit. She admits that it's haunted her ever since, wondering if he'd ever touched the younger ones. Though they show no signs of any abuse, and their progress – and specifically, the way they've answered questions – doesn't suggest they were either.'

'So that's one thing,' I said. 'But is that likely to be it now? She might get away with it?' But even as I said this I could picture the tragic figure of Mrs Gallagher. Who, despite everything, I thought genuinely did love the children, and perhaps, since she had now lost her son – well, almost as good as – she had been, and would continue to be, punished enough. And would now lose all contact with them as well. No, it wasn't as if she was a victim in the usual sense, but victim she was, even so. Could she ever have guessed, when she'd given birth to her baby son, that years later it would come down to this?

'Yes, she might. Probably will. Probably should,' Christine said. 'Would either of us want to be in her shoes? I don't think so.'

And she was right. I thought again of all her furious cake and bun baking. Who would she be able to bake cakes and buns for now? But perhaps she'd continue to do so, and send them to her son. And all the carers and warders there, maybe. Who would doubtless appreciate it. She'd have to find purpose and meaning from somewhere.

'Gawd,' I said. 'Just awful. And, no, you're right. I wouldn't. What a world we live in, eh? Come on,' I said, pushing the plate of flapjacks towards her. 'Please, give me some good news. A CAMHS appointment? A school visit? Anything?'

Christine's expression seemed to change. From one of reflection on the state of the world to one of a person who has come bearing further bad news, and hasn't been looking forward to sharing it. 'I'm so sorry to disappoint you,' she said, 'but what I have to tell you is, I'm afraid, the opposite of what I know you've been hoping for.'

I groaned. 'Oh, no. What?'

'Well, the top and bottom of it is that now Sam's disclosed, and seems to be thriving as a consequence, we've needed to put a new care plan in place.'

'And do you have any plans on the table about what this plan might involve? Because I was thinking that now he's doing so well, as you say, the best thing for him, at least in the longer short term, would be for a school place to be found as soon as possible, and locally. Yes, dependent on his assessment, because he obviously has a raft of special needs which will need supporting, but, for the moment, for us to carry on as we are. Was that the sort of plan you had in mind?'

Because I had planned. No, I hadn't exactly run it past Mike officially, but I knew that when I did he would feel the same as I did. That Sam was settled with us, used to us, responding to our programme, and with all the insecurity he'd been through, it would surely be of benefit if he could stay with us as long as he was allowed to. Possibly longer term, even. Why not?

Because.

'Not quite,' Christine said. Then sat back. 'You've grown really fond of this little one, haven't you?'

To which I wanted to explain that I fell in love with all of them – well, almost all. But we were a new team, and the only child she'd been involved in my fostering had been Miller, who'd I'd found very hard to love indeed. It had been a horrible experience. But this – this kind of painfully twanging heartstrings – was horrible too.

'Yes,' I said simply. 'I have.'

Something crossed Christine's features. Sympathy?

'Well, as I say,' she went on, 'we've had a big rethink. We're now thinking that we can forget residential schools and the like. That he's a child who could be found a forever home. You've done *such* great work with him. And who couldn't love him?'

She had a strange smile on her face. 'You mean put him up for adoption, like his siblings?'

'No, not adoption. You know how it is. He has sadly reached the age that most adoptive parents avoid, so it's not realistic to imagine that's an option.'

This was true. Most wanted younger children, and that was understandable. 'So a long-term foster family, then. But you're not thinking us.'

Christine gaped at me then. 'That's not what *you're* thinking, is it? Surely not.'

'I don't know what I'm thinking. To be honest, I've not really *been* thinking. But –'

'Keep Sam till he's eighteen! You can't think that, surely.'

'Perhaps not, but –'

She shook her head. 'That's not on the table, Casey. It can't be. Think of Tyler. And your grandkids. And the fact that if you *did* take Sam on like that, you wouldn't be able to take on any other kids, not given his high level of needs.'

I knew all of this. I had been here so many times before. And I knew I must take Christine's advice seriously. We did have Tyler, who'd legally be with us till he was eighteen, but in reality for as long as he wanted. For life, no less than that – we were family. To take Sam on too, in that way, would be a momentous decision, and not one I could or should take alone. It was a whole-family decision and whatever my gut said, my head told me differently. Sternly. We were already in our fifties, with grandkids to nurture. I thought again of Mrs Gallagher, and the sadness of her life. How lucky were we, to have all that?

'I know,' I said. 'I wasn't thinking *that* long term. I get that. I was just thinking for now.'

'But that's not fair on Sam. I don't need to tell you that.'

'No, you don't.'

'Because it would just make it all the harder when he did need to move on. No, it's a new family for Sam, without delay.'

'Yes, of course.' I thought of Sam and how he wanted to call me Mummy. How quickly it could seem as if this *was* his forever home. How hard it was going to be for him to understand why he must leave us. How hard the whole bloody kit and caboodle of it all – of saying goodbye to him – was going to be for *me*.

'So, going back to what I was saying,' Christine said, with Mary Poppins-like briskness, 'you see what a predicament we are all in? Neither CAMHS nor any school will even consider seeing him until he's in his long-term placement and settled there. It would be pointless to do any of that till then, as you know. And, besides, there's still the small possibility that he won't be in this area, in which case he'd need to be assigned to a whole new team.'

'So he might lose Colin too?' I asked. Though it wasn't really a question. Unless they found a home locally, of *course* he'd lose Colin. And would they find him somewhere locally? Unlikely. There were so many kids needing forever homes, and so few forever homes available. Try as I might – and I did – to avoid politics, you'd have to be living under a rock to avoid knowing that, increasingly, the numbers didn't work. For some, fostering challenging children long term was a vocation. But not for enough. So chances were that he'd be spirited away, far away. That was just the way it was.

'Yes,' Christine said. 'He might lose Colin. But maybe not. I really hope not. And so does he.'

Now it was my turn to gape. 'So he's in on this too? And what *is* this? Have you someone in mind yet?'

Her expression changed again. Was she toying with me? 'Possibly,' she said. 'I hope probably.'

'As in who?'

'As in a couple who are currently considering it as an option.'

'Already?' I was obviously as far out of the loop as it was possible to be.

'Already. Which is where you come in. I met with them yesterday. Lovely couple. With an "in for a penny in for a pound" mindset.' Now she leaned forward. 'Casey, they're the couple who are caring for Sam's siblings.'

If Christine had had a moustache I was sure she would have twirled it. As it was she didn't, so instead she simply lifted one hand, crossed her fingers and grinned at me.

'I had a cunning plan,' she explained. 'And it might just come off. They've been fully briefed and they're certainly up for giving it a go. So, first a visit, then a couple of sleepovers, obviously, then –'

'Hang on. Hang *on*. You mean this has already been put in place?'

'I hope so.'

'Just like that?'

'No, not quite. They were going to have him in the first place, don't forget.'

'How exactly could I forget something I didn't know?'

'Oh, yes, that had been the plan. When the children were removed they were primed to take all three of them. They're childless, sadly. Keen to make a family. Always happy to be considered for a sibling placement. It was never their decision to leave Sam out of the equation; that was our call, following the younger ones' distress at him going with them. Hence Steve and Kelly having to step in. And you know what he was like then – more than I did. More than they did. Hindsight is wonderful, but at the time of his removal, remember, it was genuinely thought that he was so mentally unstable, so feral, that *no* home environment would work for him.' She smiled. 'Casey, I don't think you realise just how far you've come with him. And now we know what we know, it changes everything, doesn't it? He *should* be with his siblings.'

'Obviously,' I agreed. 'Of course he should be with them. That was one of the reasons I was happy for him to go to Maureen Gallagher's. So there was a chance that he could still have some contact. Wow,' I said. 'Genuinely. I'm almost lost for words.'

'No words required,' she said. 'You know what I said the other day about how quickly things can change in this game?'

I sure did. That was how we got Sam in the first place. Not the troubled teen we'd been expecting. Not the mini-break. Sam. And as suddenly as he'd come to us he'd be leaving us?

It seemed so.

'Well, there you have it,' Christine said as – ugh – she gulped down the last of her cold tea. 'So brace yourself. Because this here is what's known as the game changer.'

Chapter 25

When Christine left, I spent a few minutes back at the table, just sitting. Reflecting on the tornado that had swept me up all those weeks back and whisked me off, tossed and buffeted, to Planet Sam. That's so often how it goes, particularly with a child who needs your all. You put your life on hold for a bit – how long had it been now, just shy of four months? And then, at some point, you are dropped back down to earth.

I don't know why it felt like such a bump on this occasion, because I knew this was exactly how it often happened. Had happened to me, before, certainly, when something seismic changed the game – the ying to the yang of the other kind of parting; where a child was moved on in gentle stages, to a new forever family, and we all had time and space to adjust to that change.

Not so in this case. But in one of the best ways – Sam reunited with his siblings. A new Sam, a happier Sam, a Sam who'd been unburdened. A Sam who I didn't doubt, once the plan was set before him, would embrace it unreservedly and, even if he did fret about leaving us for a bit, would immediately feel the benefits of having his family restored to him. No, not his mother, but his kin, his blood brother and sister. And if I believed anything was set in stone – well, as much as it could be in the complicated world of human relationships – it was that the bond between brothers and sisters was one of the bedrocks of a person's security. They could depend upon it into adulthood, and way, way beyond. Just as it always comforted me to know so could Riley and Kieron. Yes, they had their own family units now, and those were obviously sacrosanct, but that bond between them would never break; they would be there for each other always – including the time in their lives when Mike and I were long gone.

So though I felt a little shell-shocked that the fostering rug had been pulled out from under me so suddenly, I couldn't be anything less than thrilled for our tornado child.

Which was not to say that I didn't feel a smidgen of pique about everything. I knew it was what it was – my role was to look after Sam, day to day, and theirs was to decide what was best for him – but though I accepted that my input was a big part of that (those endless three-page daily emails that were my forte) it still rankled that, when it came to it, I didn't get a seat at the big table, and be in on the strategy-deciding stage.

So I did what I always did in moments of such irritation. I called Mike at work and had a bit of a moan.

'But, love, this is *great* news,' Mike told me. Irritatingly. 'It's the best outcome imaginable. There is not a single downside.'

I agreed. But I didn't say that. 'Well, unless it doesn't work out,' I pointed out. 'And he's brought back to us, all dejected and angry again.'

'Love, you know that's not going to happen. Why on earth would it? Sam's a changed kid. Already was, even before everything came out. You've done wonders. *We've* done wonders. The *programme* has done wonders. What on earth makes you think it will all go tits up now? Yes,' he went on, before I had a chance to rummage around for an answer, 'if he was being moved on to a new family, that would be a consideration, because he'd obviously feel, yet again, that he'd been abandoned with strangers. But that's not the case, is it? He's going back to his own family. Yes, unfamiliar carers, but living side by side with his own flesh and blood. I think he's going to thrive, I really do.'

'I know,' I conceded. 'It *is* the best outcome. I just wish they'd run it by *me* first.'

'Because it's knocked you for six,' he said. 'Because you thought we'd be hanging on to Sam for a bit longer. But mostly because of FOMO.'

'*What*?'

'Fear of missing out,' he began.

'Mike, I know what FOMO means, thank you very much.'

'Then you should recognise it in yourself, love. You just can't bear not being consulted.'

'Justifiably – who exactly has been doing all the hard work here?'

Mike burst out laughing. 'Oh, you're priceless,' he said, a tone that was *far* too jaunty. 'Love, you're not the queen of the kingdom! You can't be at the centre of *every* universe. I tell you what – I should give you my PowerPoint presentation. So you can understand management struc-tures, deployment of resources, chains of comm–'

'Right, that's it!' I huffed. 'Now I'm going to put the phone down.'

Mike blew me a kiss. 'Love you!' he sang.

I put the phone down, feeling much better. I knew it would do the trick.

Because Kieron and Sam hadn't yet returned from their football, I then took the opportunity to call Colin for a debrief. (See, Mike, I thought, I already *know* all your management jargon.) Not so much because I needed to particularly, more that I could put my marker down. After all, it was me who'd mostly be in charge of the process – more jargon – 'on the ground'.

But it seemed I was wrong there as well. 'Ah, hi Casey,' he said. 'Were your ears burning or something? I've just come off the phone to Christine, and she's filled me in on your meeting. So I was thinking I could come over for a bit – perhaps tomorrow? – so we can tell Sam the good news, and get it organised ASAP. Jim and Debbie are pretty cool with early next week. Even the weekend, if it doesn't interfere with any plans.'

'"Jim and Debbie"?'

'As in "Jim and Debbie, the new carers".'

'Oh, yes, of course,' I said quickly. Thinking 'harrumph', and more. 'Um, well, yes. Yes, that's fine. Do you want to take him off somewhere to talk, then?'

'No, not at all. I was thinking we could tell him together. Maybe take him to the park? Maybe with Flame? Would your neighbour be okay with that? Or maybe to that pub again? As a treat? I really don't mind. It's your call, this. You're the boss.'

Finally, I thought, reining my 'harrumphs' in just a little. 'I wish,' I said. 'But yes, either of those ideas is fine. As for the visit, I'm pretty free. Will these be at family centre initially?'

'Yes, the first one will, of course. But we're hoping we can get him round there sooner rather than later. No point dragging things out. Full immersion as soon as practicable, really. But you don't need to worry,' he added. 'I'll be doing all of that.'

'*You'll* be taking him?'

'Yes.'

'You don't want me to?' I asked, not adding 'because that's what usually happens'.

'No, no, I'm going to. It seemed best, given the circumstances. I'll obviously be continuing with him, so we felt it best that I support him through this process.'

Which I absolutely agreed with, but couldn't quite say. *God*, I thought, *I'm actually feeling jealous here.*

'Yes, of course it is,' I managed eventually.

'What's supernumerary?' Sam asked. 'Is it a superhero power or something?'

It was the following afternoon, and we were indeed in the local park. We'd both felt that, since it was such a gorgeous sunny day, it would be nigh on criminal to be sitting at a table, in the dark, by a big indoor play area. Open space was the thing. Room for Sam and Flame to play.

And now he'd rocked up, just as Colin and I were having another, more thoughtful debrief. And I'd surprised myself by opening up to him – this lad half my age – about the feelings that came with the ending of a placement, especially when an end, even if a good end, turned up so suddenly. 'It's just that difficult feeling of going from being at the centre of everything to suddenly being no longer needed,' I'd mused.

'I remember my mum saying that when I went off to uni,' he said. 'She said it was like she'd been made redundant. She wasn't, of course –' he added, grinning. 'Yes, I *always* took my washing home. For her sake, you understand – just to make her feel useful.'

'Mike was made redundant once,' I told him. 'I remember the letter like it was yesterday. They said he was supernumerary. We had to look it up in the dictionary.'

I turned to Sam now, who was apple-cheeked, his fringe in damp fronds. I hoped they wouldn't make him cut his hair. At least not yet. 'No,' I said, 'not a superpower. Actually the opposite of a superpower. It's like when there are so many superheroes that they have more than they need. So they have a spare one knocking about, with nothing to do. And when that happens, he or she would be known as "supernumerary".'

Sam thought for a moment. 'So it's a real word?'

'Absolutely.'

'So it really happens?'

'I suppose it could do.'

He shook his head. 'I don't think so. There can't *ever* be too many superheroes, can there, Sampson?' There's *way* not enough.'

No, there aren't, I thought. And, *God, how I'm going to miss you.*

'No, you're right, there can't, mate,' he said.

I'd brought the last of the flapjacks and made up a big bottle of squash, so, once we – or rather Sam – had exhausted Flame, at least for the moment, we sat down on the grass, just on the edge of the big stand of trees, to eat and drink and rest. And to chat. About what was coming, and how exciting it was going to be, to first visit, and say hello to, and, a little while later, to go and stay with, and then, ultimately, live with Sam's brother and sister.

Colin took the lead; I was the supporting act. Which was exactly what I should be. 'So, how'd you feel about that, mate?' Colin asked Sam once he'd run through what was going to happen. I'd been watching Sam intently throughout, to try and gauge his reaction, and was reassured to see a growing excitement in his face. But there was also, I judged, a bit of understandable anxiety.

Whatever else was true, I was still convinced that Sam was on the spectrum, and this 'game change' obviously just meant more change for him.

'Like for a long time?' he asked.

'Yes, for a long time,' Colin answered.

'So leave Casey and Mike and Tyler?' He looked at me. 'Leave mummy Casey?' I swallowed hard and nodded.

'Yes,' Colin said. 'But that doesn't mean you can't keep in touch with them. You'd like that, wouldn't you, Casey?'

'Very much,' I said. Or, rather, 'Ahem, very much, sniff.' (I was, of course, fighting back tears.)

'And Flame?'

'Yes, and Flame. But it won't be for a few weeks yet. And, guess what? A little bird told me that Jim and Debbie have a dog too. And since you're going to be the oldest brother, I imagine you'll be given lots of extra dog-walking duties. You up for that?'

I sniffed again, and quietly 'harumphed'. Out of the loop *again*.

'A big dog or a little dog?' Sam asked.

'A medium-sized dog.' Colin said. 'Like Flame.'

'Good, I like medium-sized dogs the best,' Sam said.

He gulped his glass of squash down, and then stroked Flame's head.

'Did you say a few weeks yet?' he asked.

'I did,' Colin said.

'Good,' Sam said. 'Because, mummy Casey, you know my points? Will I be able to earn lots more? And get pennies for them instead of treats?'

'I don't see why not,' I said.

'Good,' he said again. 'Because I think I'm going to have to *really* buy that dolly now, aren't I? And something for Will. A backpack. I think he's going to need to have a Spider-Man backpack, like I've got. So he and me and Sampson can go on adventures. How much do you think they cost? Lots?'

There are all kinds of love, I thought, but they have one thing in common. They always, always come at a cost.

'Oh, not too much,' I said. 'I'm sure you'll be able to earn enough, sweetheart.'

He shot an arm up, skywards. 'Because – rarrr! – I'm a superhero!'

And he was.

Epilogue

Mike being Mike, he had no truck with my whimperings and, knowing me as he did, he came back from work that evening and immediately fired up the family laptop, while Sam and Tyler set the table up for tea.

'Come here, love,' he said, beckoning me to join him. 'I've spoken to the boss and booked the first week in June off. There you go,' he said, shifting it round a bit, so I could properly see the screen.

It was an airline website, open on the page that said 'choose your destination'. And a map, on which lots of little planes swooped from Britain to all over Europe.

'Pick a mini-break,' he said. 'You have five minutes to choose.'

Those last weeks with Sam – just under three, as it turned out – went as well as anyone could have hoped for. There were two meetings at the family centre, then a day spent with his new family, then a sleepover, then a weekend, then the day came for him to move in permanently

– complete with the dolly he'd bought for Courtney and the Spider-Man backpack he'd bought for Will.

And, as sometimes happens, I never met any of them at any point. As he'd told me he would, Colin took charge of everything. Though I did, at least, write and email a few pages to my fellow carers, just to give them a flavour of what to expect, and some notes about what Sam liked and disliked.

And sometimes that's it. That's the final and only contact. You hear things, of course; bits and bobs filter down the grapevine. And as link workers and social workers know their foster carers appreciate it, they often pass on bits of news that they think we'd like to know. And sometimes the children themselves send cards or letters.

But it was rare that you had the chance to meet up with a child, and their new carers, face-to-face.

So you can imagine my joy that, with Sam, I got to do exactly that, at a big fostering event in late summer. It was a big annual party, which Mike and I sometimes, but not always, went to, held in the grounds of a mansion in the local countryside.

It was a sort of harvest festival, for foster carers and their families, where lots of fruit and vegetables were donated (we were all encouraged to 'bring a box') to be packed up later and distributed to the elderly. But with the added bonus of various outdoor games and competitions, and a concert, in which many of the attending children performed, having rehearsed for the big day for several weeks.

Ty wasn't interested in 'totes embarrassing' himself on any stage, let alone on an enormous one with a 'zillion rug rats' ('Mum, I'm nearly *seventeen* now, remember?'), and since we didn't have another child in at the time, we weren't involved in all that. But we still decided to come along, with Tyler in tow, not least because there was also a free lunch. (So don't believe what they tell you about them not existing.)

After a lovely stroll around the vast gardens, we had made our way to the drawing room inside the mansion, so we were in time to grab some good seats for the concert.

Needless to say, being the softie I am, I was immediately tearful. Not just because the children were all so sweet, which of course they were, but because they were foster children – kids who, for one reason or other, had been dealt such a bad hand, and now here they were, reciting poems, singing songs and giving thanks for the harvest. I mean, how could anyone not be moved to tears?

And then a particular group came on. On they marched, all dressed in black, with felt autumn leaves safety-pinned all over them (someone must have worked *very* hard, I thought, to get that many cut out), about twenty of them in all, cute as buttons.

Then they launched into song.

'Awww,' I whispered to Mike and Tyler, 'I just *love* this one.'

I did too. It was a classic. My own two had sung it in primary school, and my grandkids sang it too, now. It was, far and away, my favourite harvest song ever.

Ty rolled his eyes. 'Aren't you sick of hearing it?' Mike whispered.

'*Hush!*'

But then it was me being hushed, as a slender boy stepped forward, hair down to his shoulders and huge pale blue eyes.

It was Sam. Doing his solo.

'The apples are green …' he sang. 'The plums are red … The broad beans are sleeping in their blankety beds …'

It wasn't till he'd finished, and stepped back in line, that he saw us. And then he waved, a little shyly, as they finished and trooped off. And then, fifteen minutes later, dragging a bemused-looking thirty-something woman by the hand, Sam came to find us.

'Casey, Casey!' he trilled. 'Debbie, this is my mummy Casey. And Mike, and Tyler. Did you see? I got all the words right! Superstar!'

'And now a singing star as well, kiddo,' Mike told him, laughing.

'No, a *rock* star,' Tyler corrected him. '*Way* cooler.'

Introductions were made, and greetings exchanged, and we finally got to meet a rather bemused Will and Courtney, who were, to my delight, really the spit of their big brother. And as the children trotted off to play we had the chance for a catch-up, in which we heard that, so far, all was going well. Sam was in a new school – the same as his younger brother and sister, and which had an excellent special needs department to support the challenges of his autism. He was just about to return, to his new Year 5 class.

'And as Colin might have told you,' Debbie said, 'the wheels are finally turning. Fingers crossed, by this time next year, it'll all be done and dusted.'

'What will?' I asked.

'The adoption. Didn't you know?'

No,' I said. 'I mean, that's *brilliant* news. But, no, no, I didn't.'

Then, seeing Mike's face, and Ty's face, and to the astonishment of Debbie (who must have thought I was mad), I burst out laughing.

Because, honestly, what else *can* you do?

CASEY WATSON

One woman determined to make a difference.

Read Casey's poignant memoirs and be inspired.

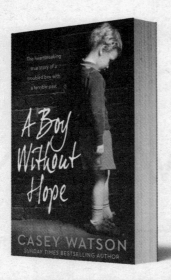

A history of abuse
and neglect has left
Miller destined for
life's scrap heap

Miller's destructive
behaviour will push Casey
to her limits, but she is
determined to help him
overcome his demons
and give him hope.

A BOY WITHOUT HOPE

Keeley is urgently
rehomed with Casey
after accusing her foster
father of abuse

It's Casey's job to keep
Keeley safe, but can
she protect this strong-
willed teen from the
dangers online?

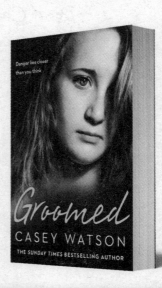

GROOMED

Bella's father is on a ventilator, fighting for his life, while her mother is currently on remand in prison, charged with his attempted murder

Bella is the only witness.

THE SILENT WITNESS

Adrianna arrives on Casey's doorstep with no possessions, no English and no explanation

It will be a few weeks before Casey starts getting the shocking answers to her questions . . .

RUNAWAY GIRL

Leo isn't a bad lad, but his frequent absences from school mean he's on the brink of permanent exclusion

Leo is clearly hiding something, and Casey knows that if he is to have any kind of future, it's up to her to find out the truth.

MUMMY'S LITTLE SOLDIER

Flip is being raised by her alcoholic mother, and comes to Casey after a fire at their home

Flip has Foetal Alcohol Syndrome (FAS), but it soon turns out that this is just the tip of the iceberg . . .

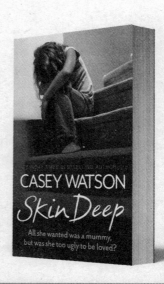

SKIN DEEP

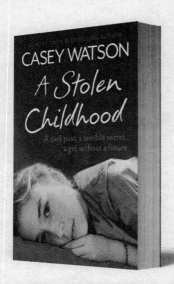

Kiara appears tired and distressed, and the school wants Casey to take her under her wing for a while

On the surface, everything points to a child who is upset that her parents have separated. The horrific truth, however, shocks Casey to the core.

A STOLEN CHILDHOOD

Eleven-year-old Tyler has stabbed his stepmother and has nowhere to go

With his birth mother dead and a father who doesn't want him, what can be done to stop his young life spiralling out of control?

NOWHERE TO GO

What is the secret behind Imogen's silence?

Discover the shocking and devastating past of a child with severe behavioural problems.

THE GIRL WITHOUT A VOICE

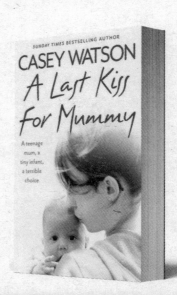

A teenage mother and baby in need of a loving home

At fourteen, Emma is just a child herself – and one who's never been properly mothered.

A LAST KISS FOR MUMMY

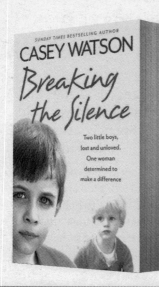

Two boys with an
unlikely bond

With Georgie and
Jenson, Casey is facing
her toughest test yet.

BREAKING THE SILENCE

A young girl secretly
caring for her mother

Abigail has been dealing
with pressures no child
should face. Casey has the
difficult challenge of helping
her to learn to let go.

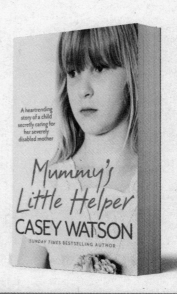

MUMMY'S LITTLE HELPER

Branded 'vicious and evil', eight-year-old Spencer asks to be taken into care

Casey and her family are disgusted: kids aren't born evil. Despite the challenges Spencer brings, they are determined to help him find a loving home.

TOO HURT TO STAY

Abused siblings who do not know what it means to be loved

With new-found security and trust, Casey helps Ashton and Olivia to rebuild their lives.

LITTLE PRISONERS

CASEY WATSON

Crying for Help

The shocking story of a damaged girl with a dark past

A damaged girl haunted by her past

Sophia pushes Casey to the limits, threatening the safety of the whole family. Can Casey make a difference in time?

CRYING FOR HELP

Five-year-old Justin was desperate and helpless

Six years after being taken into care, Justin has had 20 failed placements. Casey and her family are his last hope.

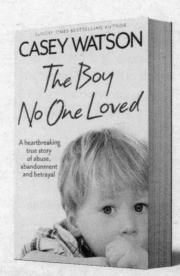

CASEY WATSON

The Boy No One Loved

A heartbreaking true story of abuse, abandonment and betrayal

THE BOY NO ONE LOVED

AVAILABLE AS E-BOOK ONLY

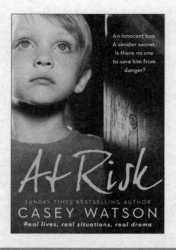

Adam is brought to Casey while his mum recovers in hospital – just for a few days

But a chance discovery reveals that Casey has stumbled upon something altogether more sinister . . .

AT RISK

Six-year-old Darby is naturally distressed at being removed from her parents just before Christmas

And when the shocking and sickening reason is revealed, a Happy New Year seems an impossible dream as well . . .

THE LITTLE PRINCESS

AVAILABLE AS E-BOOK ONLY

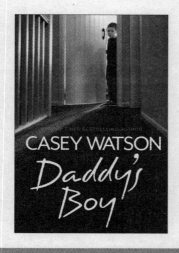

Paulie, just five, is a boy out of control – or is he just misunderstood?

The plan for Paulie is simple: get him back home with his family. But perhaps 'home' isn't the best place for him . . .

DADDY'S BOY

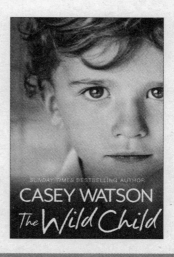

Angry and hurting, eight-year-old Connor is from a broken home

As streetwise as they come, he's determined to cause trouble. But Casey is convinced there is a frightened child beneath the swagger.

THE WILD CHILD

AVAILABLE AS E-BOOK ONLY

Nathan has a sometime alter ego called Jenny who is the only one who knows the secrets of his disturbed past

But where is Jenny when she is most needed?

NO PLACE FOR NATHAN

Jade and Scarlett, seventeen-year-old twins, share a terrible secret

Can Casey help them come to terms with the truth and rediscover their sibling connection?

SCARLETT'S SECRET

AVAILABLE AS E-BOOK ONLY

Cameron is a sweet boy who seems happy in his skin – making him rather different from most of the other children Casey has cared for

But what happens when Cameron disappears? Will Casey's worst fears be realised?

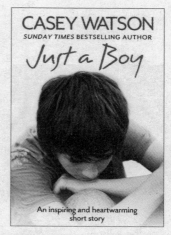

JUST A BOY

FEEL HEART.
FEEL HOPE.
READ CASEY.

Discover more about Casey Watson.
Visit www.caseywatson.co.uk

Find Casey Watson on &

Moving Memoirs

Stories of hope, courage and the power of love…

If you loved this book, then you will love our
Moving Memoirs eNewsletter

Sign up to…

- Be the first to hear about new books

- Get sneak previews from your favourite authors

- Read exclusive interviews

- Be entered into our monthly prize draw to win one
  of our latest releases before it's even hit the shops!

Sign up at

www.moving-memoirs.com